Happy Birthday Nancy — !

Love,
Betty, Bob & Wayne
1961

Wilton's
WONDERLAND
OF CAKE DECORATING

Authors: McKINLEY WILTON & NORMAN WILTON

FIRST EDITION
Copyright 1960
by
McKINLEY WILTON AND NORMAN WILTON

CHICAGO INTERNATIONAL TRADE FAIR
*Official Cake**

* Three days were spent in decorating and assembling this project.

This gigantic confection was six feet tall, in seven tiers on a 44″ base and created especially for the Chicago International Trade Fair. The cake was unveiled in advance for the benefit of the Press, TV, and Radio, sent across the wires on nation-wide releases, and reached many of the various papers throughout the country. The cake was devoted to the theme of the International Trade Fair, "the St. Lawrence Seaway", and "Chicago as a Transportation Center and Major World Port."

Assembled in four sections, it was wired with soft rosebud electric lights shining through decorated cake icing. The bottom tier was a reproduction of the St. Lawrence Seaway, with four freighters sailing around the cake, and a ship being unloaded by a large crane. The third tier represented Chicago as a railroad center with a locomotive pulling freight cars. Under the first tier surrounded by pillars of cake icing was a model F707 Jet plane symbolizing Chicago's importance in the jet age.

On top of the cake was a 14″ globe of the world made of multi-colored icing which revolved under soft lighting. Each country of the world was outlined in a different color, with the United States in gold and Chicago spotted with a flag, emblazoned with the Chicago International Trade Fair. The flags of 42 nations were placed around the base of the cake. This cake was on display in the lobby of the Inland Steel building in downtown Chicago and was the official cake for the opening of the Chicago International Trade Fair.

Published by

McKINLEY WILTON AND NORMAN WILTON
Wilton Enterprises, Inc. 11010 S. Halsted St.
Chicago 28, Ill.

Dedicated to our

(bosses, the homemakers, who delight in the fulfillment of creating beauty in the home.)

1st printing, March 1960 — 15,000
2nd printing, September 1960 — 15,000

The authors wish to thank

Mort Witz, Chicago, Ill., for his photographic work.
The Schram Advertising Company, Chicago, Illinois,
for, their valuable assistance in preparing this book.

MR. McKINLEY WILTON . . . world's most renowned Cake Decorator and Fine Candy Maker. Founder and President of the famous Wilton School of Cake Decorating and Fine Candy Making. Originator of the Modern Techniques of Master Cake Decorating and Pulled Sugar Work.

Mr. Norman Wilton...Nationally Known Consultant, Lecturer and Demonstrator of Modern Cake Decorating Techniques, Pulled Sugar Artistry and Fine Candy Making. Vice-President and Instructor of the Wilton School.

Table of Contents

SECTION   PAGES

I   INTRODUCTION, THE WILTON SCHOOL 8, 9

II   DECORATING ICINGS 10, 11

III   ORNAMENTING TIPS AND CONES 12-14

IV   DROP FLOWERS AND LEAVES 15, 16

V   ROYAL ICING 17

VI   COLOR TECHNIQUES 18-20

VII   DECORATED CAKES—WEDDING, ANNIVERSARY,
      RELIGIOUS, SPECIAL OCCASION, NOVELTY
      AND CHILDREN'S 23, 36-43, 79-83, 89-91,
                                                   94, 99-121, 124, 138, 139

VIII CAKE BORDERS 24-35

IX   SUGAR MOLD 44-46

X   EASTER DECORATIONS AND CHRISTMAS ORNAMENTS 49, 50

XI   FIGURE PIPING 51

XII   LATTICE DESIGNS 74-76, 122, 125

XIII STYROFOAM—FORMS, CONFECTIONS AND PATTERNS . . . 77, 78, 134-137, 140-146

XIV   GUM PASTE AND INSTANT FONDANT 84-88

XV   CENTERPIECES 92

XVI   SCENERY PAINTING 126

XVII KNICKNACK PARTY CAKE DECORATIONS 127-133

XVIII GREETING CARDS 147, 148

XIX   ICE CARVING 149, 150

XX   GRADUATION AND STUDENTS CAKE 151

Introduction

Wilton's wonderland of cake decorating, is to be regarded as a sequel to our first book, The Beginners Instruction Book, Homemakers Pictorial Encyclopedia of Modern Cake Decorating. This book opens the door to a galaxy of new and easy ideas, new methods, new materials and equipment. We are sure the cake decorating homemaker will literally want to dive right in. As usual, all of our ideas are easily assembled or decorated, as the case may be. No need to be a mastermind to turn out this myriad of delightful confections.

We are able to accommodate you on any of the accessories through our mail order supply. For information on supplies write: Wilton Enterprises, 11010 S. Halsted, Chicago 28, Illinois.

Guess there is not much else to say but, Have fun!

THE WILTON SCHOOL

The teaching record of the Wilton school is the greatest endorsement of the Wilton method and the Wilton standing in the cake decorating and fine candy making field.

Not only have over 4,000 professional bakers attended the school but the student body is also comprised of thousands of hotel chefs, home economists, home-arts teachers, dieticians, hobbyists and homemakers.

Students have come from every state in the Union and from many foreign countries as well.

Periodically the Wilton School "takes to the road" and travels world-wide to hold classes. Wilton classes have been held in Hawaii, Japan, India, and in most of the countries in Europe.

DECORATING ICINGS

Realizing the housewife has many favorite frostings for her cakes we will concentrate on decorating icings.

No matter how you practice decorating and how much equipment you have, your icing must be at the right consistency or all your decorating efforts will be in vain.

When working with a decorating icing, it is often necessary to vary the consistency of your particular icing. If you are practicing a simple border, your icing should be of a medium consistency. For many of the different types of flowers, a stiffer icing is required in order to make the petal stand up and have a more lifelike effect. All of our decorating formulas are worked out to give you a medium stiff consistency and they may be used for either flowers or borders. Where you are told to thin down the icing slightly, do so by adding a few drops of water. Now the question arises, where would a thinned down icing be used? In string work and tube writing the icing must be of a thinner consistency in order to draw out properly. If a heavy, stiff icing is used, as pressure is applied to the cone the icing will tend to break as it is moved along the surface of the cake. By using a thinner icing it will tend to string out and much better results will be obtained. It is very important that you follow our icing recipes in detail, for without the proper icing or the proper consistency all of your practice and our instructions will be in vain.

There are three main types of decorating icing. The *buttercream*, the *boiled* and *royal* icing.

All of the following icings were tested on a standard home electric mixer. Heavy duty mixers will require 3 to 4 minutes less beating time per each step. It is important to remember all utensils must be completely free of grease.

Keep in mind that these icings are for decorating and must be stiff. If you are using the proper ingredients there are only two things that would make your icing fail: 1. Not beating long enough
2. A tiny amount of grease in your batch.

WILTON SPECIAL BUTTERCREAM ICING RECIPE

1 lb. powdered sugar
¼ lb. butter, margarine or shortening
2¾ ounces evaporated milk
¼ teaspoon of butter flavor (if shortening is used)
½ teaspoon vanilla
pinch of salt.
Mix all ingredients together and beat for 5 minutes at medium speed. By using butter in the icing you get a tastier flavor. By using shortening, your buttercream will be much lighter in color. If you wish to thin the consistency of the icing, do so by adding a few drops of evaporated milk. This would be the consistency for icing a cake.
This is a smooth, tasty, easily made buttercream icing that may be used for flower and border work, also for decorating ice cream pies and any type of sweets you wish to freeze.

WILTON'S SPECIAL NEW FORMULA DECORATORS BOILED ICING

(A) *7 level teaspoons of Wilton De Luxe Meringue Powder*
6 ounces of hot water (not boiling)

(B) *3 cups granulated sugar*
5 ounces of water
½ teaspoon cream of tarter

Dissolve "A" in measuring cup. Pour into your 4 quart mixing bowl and beat at high speed about 8 minutes.
Place "B" in a deep sauce pan and cook to 240°. To get the proper temperature reading, your thermometer must be covered by at least 2 inches of mixture.
Wash sides of pan down while mixture is boiling, using warm water and a brush. This will remove the crystals from the sides of pan.
When "B" has reached 240° pour slowly in a thin thread to mixture "A" while beating at high speed until icing holds a peak, about 10 minutes. Add flavoring as desired. If you wish to make up flowers in advance and dry for future use, place on a cookie sheet in a 200° oven for one hour.

DECORATING BUTTER CREAM

1 cup vegetable shortening
1½ cups confectioners sugar
¼ cup evaporated milk
Cream at high speed for 5 minutes.

For tastier icing, use half butter and half shortening and replace the milk with cream.

To thin down the icing for inscriptions and borders, add a few drops of liquid. Store in airtight container in the refrigerator. Whip up before using the second time.

This is a very good decorating icing for practicing your various flowers.

Flowers made up in advance using this recipe should be placed in the refrigerator to harden slightly and become easy to handle.

FRENCH BUTTERCREAM

This is a very delicious and unusual buttercream to be used for cake or French pastries. This buttercream has as smooth a texture as whipped cream, and is really delicious.

Make a batch of either of our boiled icing recipes. Spread in sheet pan and let cool completely. Fold in (do not beat) ⅛ lb. of butter at room temperature.

If a thinner consistency is desired, add a few drops of cream.

ROYAL ICING WITH MERINGUE POWDER

3 level tablespoons of meringue powder
1 lb. of confectioners powdered sugar
3½ oz. water (slightly less than ½ cup)
½ teaspoon of cream of tartar
This is a hard drying icing and must be covered at all times with a damp cloth.

The above ingredients are placed in a mixing bowl and beaten for 7 to 10 minutes at high speed.

Use this icing when you are making up flowers or various decorations in advance. The icing will dry and you may peel it off your waxed paper and place your decorations on cakes, petits fours, etc. without damaging your decorations.

Because of its hard drying qualities it is also used to fasten together icing or sugar mold work. You may re-beat this icing the following day and it will regain its original consistency.

For a lighter icing, add a tablespoon of water and continue beating. The addition of water and continued beating makes this icing even lighter than boiled icing. When your flowers harden from this lightly beaten icing, they must be handled very carefully because the air cells in the icing tend to crumble.

ROYAL ICING MADE WITH EGG WHITE

3 egg whites (room temperature)
1 lb. confectioners sugar
½ teaspoon cream of tartar
The above ingredients are placed in mixing bowl and beaten for 7 to 10 minutes.

This icing is a hard drying icing. Keep covered with damp cloth at all times.

This is used in the same way as the Royal icing with meringue powder, but it will not give as much volume and will not beat up as well for use at a later date.

BOILED ICING WITH MERINGUE POWDER

(A) 4 level tablespoons of meringue powder.
    ½ cup of water.
(B) 2 cups granulated sugar.
    ½ cup water.
    ¼ teaspoon cream of tartar.
(C) 1 lb. confectioners sugar (powdered).

Mix "A" together by pouring water into bowl and adding meringue powder. Beat at high speed for 7 minutes. Put "B" ingredients in a saucepan and boil until a temperature of 240 degrees is reached. Wash sides of pan down while mixture is boiling, using warm water and a brush. This will remove the crystals from the sides of the pan.

While sugar is boiling turn beater to low speed and add "C". Then turn to high speed and beat for 4 minutes. When "B" reaches 240 degrees add it slowly to mixture "A" and "C". Then beat at high speed for 5 minutes, and add desired flavoring.

When you use this type of boiled icing you may keep it for as long as a week. Keep in refrigerator with damp cloth over the top of bowl. Simply beat up before re-using. It is not necessary to add anything when re-beating.

This type of icing is perfect for flowers and border work. It will not weep or run in any weather. Keep covered with a damp cloth at all times to prevent crusting.

BOILED ICING USING EGG WHITES

(A)
2 cups granulated sugar.
½ cup of water.
¼ teaspoon of cream of tartar.

(B)
4 egg whites (at room temperature).

(C)
1½ cups of confectioners sugar, and sift. Cook "A" to 240 degrees. When it starts to boil do not let mixture crystallize on the sides of the pan. You can prevent this from happening by washing the sides of the pan down with warm water and a brush. Repeat the washing-down process about halfway through being careful *not* to stir the batch.

While the sugar is boiling place "B" in a mixing bowl and whip at high speeds for 7 minutes. Pour "A" in slowly and whip for 3 minutes more. Turn down to second speed and add "C" gradually. Turn back to high speed and whip the entire contents for 5 minutes more.

You will not be able to rebeat this icing on the following day and have it regain its stiff consistency as you do when using our meringue powder.
Keep covered with damp cloth while using.

11

ORNAMENTING TIPS AND THEIR USES

Ornamenting tips are the basic tools used for decorating cakes and general ornamenting, although there are nearly 200 tips in use today, all practical needs are met through the use of a few tips. Throughout this book, we are going to elaborate on the uses of various and specialty decorating tips.

Bear in mind that the decorating tip is not the most important thing in cake decorating. The person behind the tip—the person squeezing the bag is the important factor as far as making flowers and borders is concerned. Keeping this in mind, you can see the decorating skill comes from careful pressure control—the squeezing and relaxing of pressure on the cone. With smooth, co-ordinated movements of the nail and cone almost any flower can be made. The same holds true with all border work designs.

Any type of material may be used for decorations as long as it flows through the cone or tip, and will hold a shape. In preparing your various materials for decorating, keep in mind the consistency of your icings. If the substance goes through the tip and loses its form, it is too thin. If too much pressure is required to push it through the tip, then your substance must be thinned down slightly. With this in mind, we shall proceed with the uses of the tip in making many variations of border work.

Many of the basic elementary steps in border work will not be covered in this book, because all of our beginning steps and pressure control lessons were pictured and illustrated in our Homemaker's Encyclopedia of Modern Cake Decorating by Wilton.

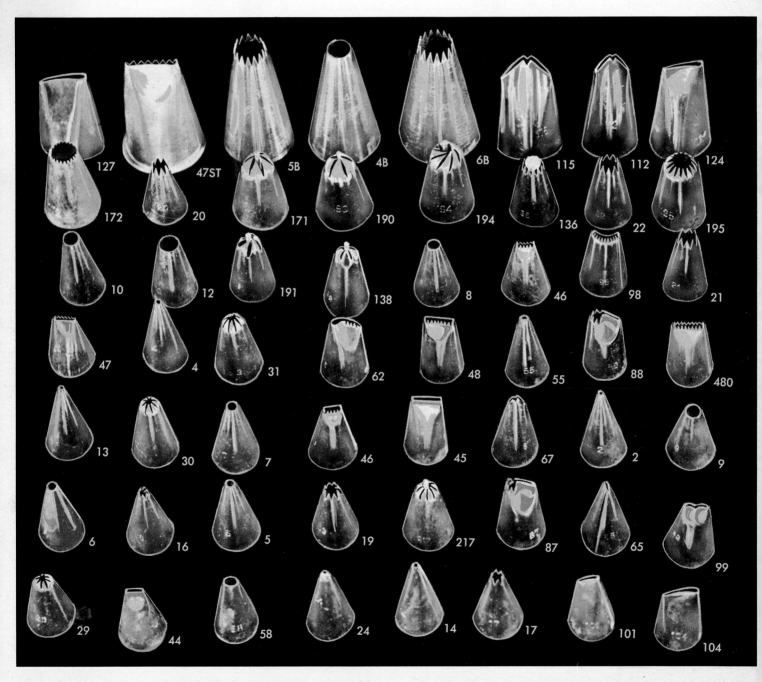

No. 7 NAIL

This is a No. 7 Flower Nail. The nail is held in the left hand using the thumb, index finger and middle finger to pivot or turn the nail. Approximately ninety-five percent of our flowers are made on this type of nail. By holding the nail in your left hand and the tube in your right hand, and squeezing the tube while turning the nail in a co-ordinated series of movements, many different flowers will be made. After the flower is made, it is lifted from the nail with a pair of scissors and placed on the cake. If the flower is to be made with a hard drying type of icing for future use, the following method is used. Cut 2 inch squares of waxed paper. Put a small dot of icing on the nail and stick the waxed paper directly to the nail. After the flower is completed, slide the square of waxed paper off the nail. Using this method any number of flowers can be made on the same nail.

No. 7 NAIL   No. 12 NAIL

No. 12 EASTER LILY NAIL

This is similar to the other nail except that it has a cup shape, and is used to make the Easter Lily. The disadvantage in a flower such as this type is that it is necessary to have one nail on each flower. The nail is greased with lard or heavy grease. The flower is made of royal icing inside the nail cup. When the flower is dry, it is lifted out of the cup.

CONSTRUCTING A PAPER CONE AND APPLICATION

Having discussed the tubes and their various uses, the next problem is constructing a cone together with the proper method of holding a cone and the correct way to squeeze it. Decorating cones are used in the following order: Paper cones are used by professionals, canvas and rubber cones by some bakers, and a metal cylinder and plunger is strictly for the housewife and has a very limited use. The one thing that discourages the beginner from using paper is not knowing how to construct the cone properly. With five minutes practice, you can become very proficient in making a cone. Although any type of paper can be used, the best is a vegetable parchment. If this is not obtainable, waxed paper can be used. The heavier the waxed paper, the easier to construct the cone. Brown wrapping paper is satisfactory if not used for any great length of time; it absorbs up the moisture in the icing, and when your paper becomes wet, it will break.

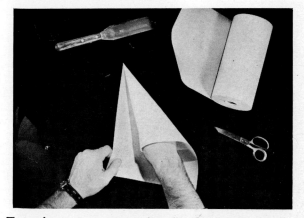

To make a paper cone using the 9 inch roll, the sheet should be approximately 17 inches long. The object is to roll the paper in the shape of a cone.

After the cone is made, the tip is cut off about ½ inch from the end, and the tube is dropped into the cone. To fill the cone with icing, the base is held in the left hand and the icing is scooped up with a spatula knife and placed into the cone.

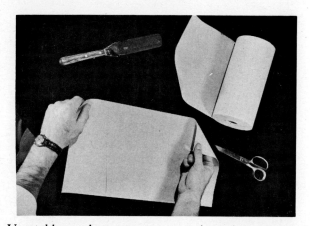

Vegetable parchment paper comes in various sizes and cuts. We normally use the 9 inch roll for most of our purposes.

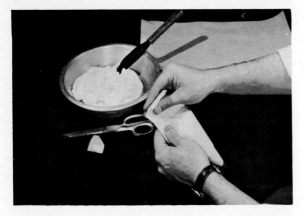

Do not fill the cone over ¾ full. After the cone is full, the top of the cone is folded in. This keeps the icing from backing out of the cone as pressure is applied. Before cutting the tip off the cone, be sure the cone is needle sharp.

Here we illustrate the proper position of the nail and the tube when constructing a rose.

For a small cone, an oblong piece of parchment paper may be cut in half and the same procedure followed using the long side of the triangle to construct the cone. As the cone becomes empty, it is necessary to continue folding the top down as the icing is forced out.

Illustrated is the position of the tube on the nail when making flowers such as the daisy, dahlia, yellow jonquil or any flower with a relatively flat petal.

Illustrated is the proper method of holding the cone while working on a cake top. The tube is held at a 45 degree angle from the surface. When using a No. 104 tube as in most of our flowers, the large end of the tube is touching the surface and the small end is standing out. Use the left hand as shown to steady the cone. This is the normal position of the cone for working on a cake.

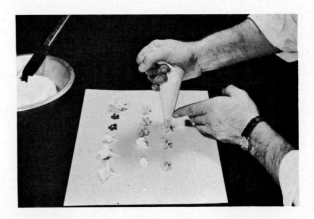

This is the position of the cone when we speak of holding the cone perpendicular to the cake. Illustrated here is the procedure in making a five petal drop flower with a single squeeze and turn.

DROP FLOWERS

These are strictly a production flower and should be made up ahead of time on sheets of waxed paper using royal icing. By changing color and centers, many different types of flowers can be made. Pink would be used for an apple blossom, white for orange blossoms and purple for the violet. Also by varying the size of the tips, again, many variations may be obtained. Make these flowers in royal icing on a sheet of waxed paper stuck to a pan with icing. The tip is rested on the waxed paper, holding the cone perpendicular to the pan. Turn the hand to the left as far as possible, then squeeze the cone and turn the hand to the right as far as possible while squeezing. This gives distinct petals with just one operation. If the petals are too thick, the pressure applied to the cone has been too heavy.

A No. 29 tip is used to make this small flower. A squeeze and a turn as described above is all that is needed.

Use a No. 136 tip for this drop flower, no turning is necessary—just squeeze and stop and the petals are formed. The center may be filled in with a contrasting color.

This is a slightly larger drop flower and is made with a No. 171 tip. Again, squeeze and turn, forming the distinct petals.

Use a No. 138 tip, and with a very small amount of pressure, a very tiny flower can be made, and used as a simulated forget-me-not. No turn is necessary for this flower, just squeeze and stop.

This drop flower is made using a No. 191 tip. The cone must be squeezed and turned in one operation to form these petals as for drop flower described previously.

A No. 217 drop flower tip is used. This tip has ten openings thus giving ten petals. It is made with a squeeze and a turn, forming the petals.

This is a little larger drop flower than the preceding flowers. A No. 194 tip is used. The flower is made with a squeeze and turn of the cone.

This particular flower is made with our old standby, the No. 190 drop flower tip. Five petals are formed by merely squeezing and turning as illustrated.

LEAVES

Making a leaf properly is as important as making most of your flowers. The essential part of making a leaf is to have the icing at the proper consistency. It must be thinned down so it may be drawn out to a point.

There are six standard size leaf tips, starting with the small size No. 65 through No. 70. The special leaf tips for extra large leaves run from No. 112 through No. 115.

Approximately 4 or 5 size leaves may be made using any one size leaf tip. Pressure control and movement of the tip is the important factor regarding a leaf size.

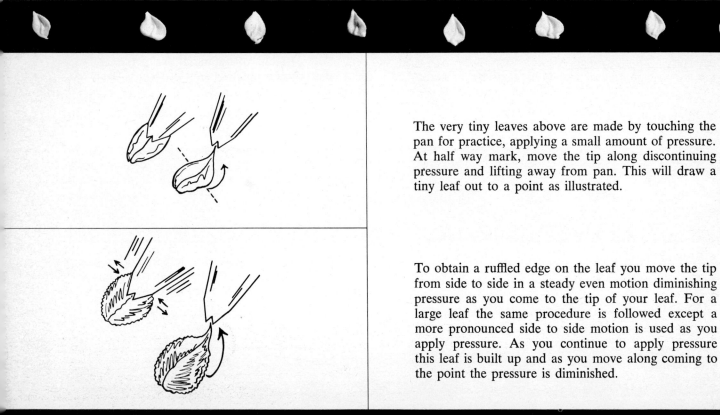

The very tiny leaves above are made by touching the pan for practice, applying a small amount of pressure. At half way mark, move the tip along discontinuing pressure and lifting away from pan. This will draw a tiny leaf out to a point as illustrated.

To obtain a ruffled edge on the leaf you move the tip from side to side in a steady even motion diminishing pressure as you come to the tip of your leaf. For a large leaf the same procedure is followed except a more pronounced side to side motion is used as you apply pressure. As you continue to apply pressure this leaf is built up and as you move along coming to the point the pressure is diminished.

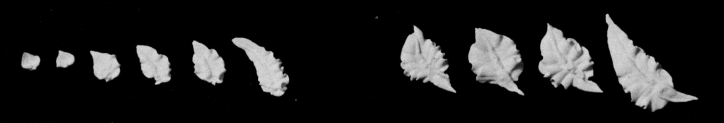

The first three leaves were made with a No. 65 tip. The second three leaves were made using a No. 67 tip.

The four leaves illustrated above were made with a No. 68 tip.

Above three leaves were made using a No. 69 tip.

The above two leaves were made using a No. 70 tip.

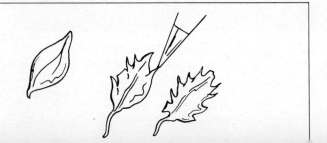

To obtain the pointed effect on the edges of the leaves, a small cone with a No. 3 tube is filled with thinned down icing. The cone is placed into the side of the leaf. A small amount of pressure is applied to the cone and as you move away discontinue pressure, thus forming the points on the leaf.

16

CHRYSANTHEMUMS

A new method of making a mum out of royal icing. These flowers may be made in advance and after drying stored away and used when the occasion arises.

Cut a hollow rubber ball in half—we used a 2⅛ " ball for our mum. The finished mum will be approximately 1″ larger than the diameter of your ball. The half ball may be placed on a turned over cup or glass for easier decorating.

The royal icing should be thinned down slightly. This will tend to give a more pointed petal. Make a larger cone and drop a No. 79 tip into the cone. Use any desired color—we used yellow icing—brush a strip of paste color down the inside of the cone and fill the cone with icing. (See color technique for paste color striping.)

Grease the ball heavily with lard. In our series of steps we did not picture this next step as it would not photograph well. Cover the entire ball with icing using any flat tube. Starting at the base of the ball a series of petals are piped on. This is done by squeezing and moving away from the ball—as you obtain the desired length of your petal relax pressure and continue moving away. This will break the petal off evenly. After completing the base row continue moving up as illustrated until the entire half section of the ball is covered. After drying the half ball is squeezed together slightly and the mum slips off.

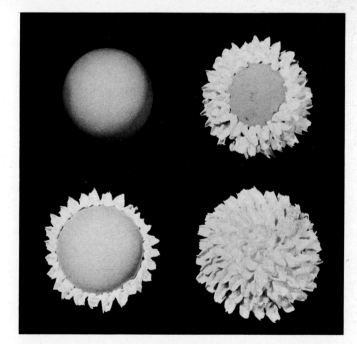

If you care to make the mum using a soft icing it may be made in the same manner only using a piece of cake for the base and rounding it out in icing.

For our finished cake we used a 8″ two layer—the cake was iced in white and trimmed in yellow using a No. 105 tip for the border and trimmed with a No. 3 tip using the scroll in green.

The series of leaves were made with a No. 70 tip.

THE IMPORTANCE OF COLOR TECHNIQUE IN MODERN CAKE DECORATING

A prime factor in increasing the sale of decorated cakes is the use of the proper color techniques. This technique, with the Wilton production methods of application reproduce in detail the exact colors, tones and values desired on the decorated cake. Originated and perfected by the Wilton School, and taught to over 4000 students during the past four years, the Wilton Color Techniques and Modern Production Methods are now available to you in this book. Read it carefully. Take advantage of these instructions to increase your sales. Modern decorated cakes are your high profit and prestige line. Here are proven and tested techniques that will tremendously increase your cake sales.

SPATULA STRIPING

This is the most usual color blending method. After placing a tube in the cone, use a small bow knife and put a one inch strip of colored icing down the entire side of the cone. After striping the cone, fill the remainder of the cone with white icing. As an example, let's say you want to make some pink and white roses. The pink will appear on the inside of the rose and the white should be out at the tips. This simulates the way nature bleaches out the rose at the tips of the petals. In this case you would strip the large side of a No. 104 tube in pink icing with a strip approximately ½ inch thick and 1 inch wide and the remainder would be filled with white icing. Then as you make your rose, the petals will be pink except for the tips which are white.

This method of striping can and should be used on borders. In making a shell border with a large star tube, the bag should have a narrow strip of colored icing on one side. The rest of the bag is filled with white icing. This gives the border a beautiful two-tone effect.

DEEP COLOR METHOD

For all decorators the problem of getting a deep red or green is almost an impossibility. By using the brush method of striping, this becomes relatively simple. First make up some medium red icing. Dip your brush into the red paste color and brush it around the entire inside of the cone. After this is completed, fill your cone with the red icing. With this method all of the coloring is on the outside of the flower or border and is not wasted on the inner part.

This method can be used for many different occasions and is not only practical but makes your colors go much further. A deep black may be used completing a snow man, or a deep yellow for the stamens of a flower.

MASKING METHODS

This method, illustrated on the opposite page in the winter scene cake, is a mass production technique similar to the use of a stencil. The desired pattern or figure is cut out of a piece of heavy cardboard. This mask can then be used over and over again. The icing may be applied with a spatula to the cake areas not covered by the mask, or colored areas may be sprayed on.

In the illustrated cake, a separate mask was used for the sky, mountains and evergreens. In producing a large number of cakes with the same design, use one on all cakes successively and then go over the cakes with the other masks in turn. After the icing or coloring has been applied by the masking method, further decoration may be accomplished by piping.

BRUSH STRIPING

This is a new idea in striping your bag with many different colors and still using a plain white icing.

For a fall leaf effect, we strip the bag with a brush in 3 places. First with brown coloring on each side, then with green in the middle. These strips should be about ⅛ of an inch wide and extend from top to bottom of the cone. After striping is completed, the cone is filled with pastel green icing. The leaves will have a beautiful three tone effect; a pastel green leaf with brown on each side and a deep green shade in the center. All of this is done simply by making 3 strips with a brush. These are the steps for a better cake business — use them!

SPRAYING METHOD

The spraying method of coloring is becoming more popular every day. In using this method, no expensive equipment is necessary. It will cost you just 40c for an atomizer at any Art store. With this simple atomizer, all of your spraying equipment is taken care of.

The flowers are made up first on wax paper in white icing. Then take a small glass of water and color it delicately with paste color. The flowers are then sprayed with the colored water with the atomizer. These flowers must be made up and sprayed before placing them on a cake. Very deep colors may be attained by simply making your water a dark color.

BLENDING PULLED SUGAR

Fall leaves, the orchid and similar decorations in pulled sugar require two or more colors. The blending of the colors is easily achieved. As an example, consider the fall leaf: A one inch strip of yellow candy is placed on top of a piece of green candy three inches in diameter. The leaf is then pulled out as described in detail under *Pulled Sugar*. As the leaf is formed, the two colors blend giving the desired effect. Another small piece of candy in a third color may be added to create pulled sugar in three blended colors.

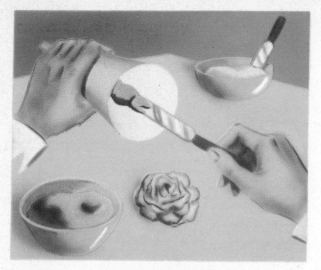

SPATULA STRIPING

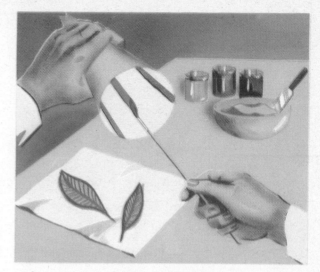

BRUSH STRIPING

DEEP COLOR METHOD

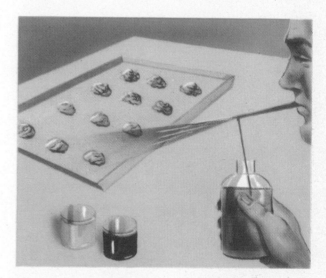

SPRAYING METHOD

MASKING METHOD

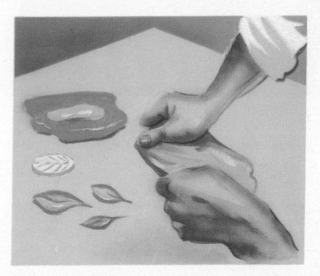

BLENDING PULLED SUGAR

MERRY-GO-ROUND CAKE

Round and round she goes and where she stops nobody knows. This colorful carrousel cake is easily assembled. Very little decorating is necessary as all the novelty items such as the umbrella, ribbon, clowns and horses are available in our mail order catalog. Ice two 10″ layer cakes. The umbrella is 9″ in diameter. It is iced with a white royal icing. The gaily colored circles are put on with a No. 3 tip and No. 3 silver dragees are used in the center of each circle. The handle of the umbrella is also iced in royal icing and then wrapped in ribbon. After sticking the umbrella through the center of the cake eight ribbons are attached using royal icing as illustrated. The colorful balls at the base of the cake are made with a No. 12 tip, by simply squeezing and relaxing pressure as you move up forming the ball. The top border is made in the same manner with a No. 6 tip. The funny dressed clowns are characters that will do anything and are fully dressed in cloth clothes with movable arms and legs that can be bent into position. After the cake is placed in the center of the party table, eight prancing horses are set in position to pull the carrousel along. When the cake is cut each child at the party receives a little horse for his very own.

THE RAMBLING ROSE

This is a 14, 12, 9 and 6″ wedding cake. The cake is iced in butter cream and decorated in boiled icing. The roses are made in royal icing and after drying, placed on the cake in the following manner. After each rose is dry it is lifted off the waxed paper and using a No. 30 star tip, a small point is piped at the base of each rose.

After this dries the roses are stuck into the cake in a long circular manner starting at the base and working up. This royal icing point will help fasten the rose to the cake. Lily of the valley and silver leaves are then worked in to finish this spray.

ELABORATE STYLING

This distinctive looking wedding cake is made up of three tiers, a separation, and then two tiers. Starting at the base, we use an 18″ square, a 14″ round, 11″ round, a number 500-8-5″ high separation, 9″ round and a 6″ round. As mentioned in our paragraph on cakes, we suggest a tier to be made of three layers and the base tier of 4 layers.

The cake is placed on a 22″ wooden board covered with gold doilies. The No. 500-8-5″ grecian separation is also sprayed with a gold color. Such a spray can be purchased at hardware stores and is in a pressurized can.

The large shell border around the base is made with a No. 5B tip. The draped garland with fluted edge around the side of the base border is made with a No. 124 tip.

A No. 48° tip is used in a series of back and forth motions directly above the No. 124 fluted edge. A No. 8 tip is used for the heavy string work directly under the fluted edge and a No. 5 tip is used for the double drop loop and the draped garland. A medium sized bell mold WB 5 is used to form the sugar bells above the bottom tier. All shell borders on this large cake are made with a No. 21 star tip. The heavier string work is made with a No. 5 tip and the thinner string work on the upper portions of the cake is made with a No. 3 tip.

The only flowers on the cake are the sweet peas which are made up ahead of time in royal icing and after drying enough for handling are placed on the cake as shown. The lily of the valleys are artificial.

Two sizes of gold leaves are used on the wedding cake. The large leaf is our No. 62 gold leaf and the small leaf is our No. 67 gold leaf.

A cake of this size will serve approximately 400 people, nicely.

CAKE BORDERS

Aside from the attractiveness of the borders themselves, they perform the function of smoothing the cake edges and covering the flaws and defects of icing, etc. They finish the cake by giving it a uniform appearance. There is a tendency among the inexperienced cake decorators to invent all sorts of reasons why many borders are "impractical" to use, this is because many of the borders look as though they may be difficult to execute. Actually, some of the most intricate looking borders are simple to make. It is hoped that the reader of this book will at least try out all of the borders shown on these pages. Once you have tried them you will see they are not complicated, not difficult and not even too time consuming. They will be a great asset to any housewife who really wants to create beautifully decorated cakes.

We will not go into detail explaining basic borders as we feel most of you will have worked from our first book and acquired many of the basic steps of cake decorating. With proper pressure and manipulation of the cone, almost any design imaginable can be made. Nearness, working closely enough to the cake so the icing doesn't stretch or break—and yet far enough away so it doesn't bunch up or bulk. Uniformity of design is essential. Master these and your borders will become a series of simple steps which you can execute simply and with precision.

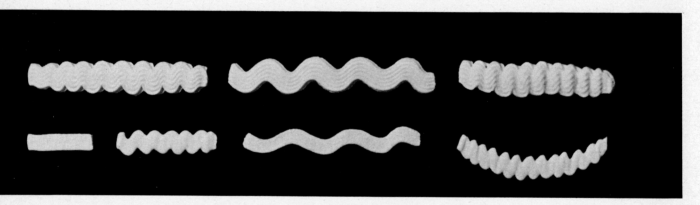

ZIG ZAG BORDER

This is a good practice exercise and depending on the tip used, many variations of designs may be executed. Beginning with the top row a No. 47 tip is used. The cone is held at a 45° angle to the surface. Start with an even, steady pressure on the cone while moving in a short side to side motion. The second border in the top row is made by using the same tip, only the side to side motion is more gentle thus giving a relaxed ripple effect. The third section again is made with a No. 47 tip but with a quick back and forth movement, changing the appearance completely from the other three borders.

The bottom row is made with a No. 44 tip. The first section is drawn out in a straight line. The second section using the same tip is a series of back and forth motions. The third section similar to the top is a more relaxed drawn out pressure. The fourth section is a series of fine back and forth motions again using the No. 44 tip.

DROP FLOWER BORDER

Using a No. 172 tip, fill a cone ½ full of icing. Hold the cone perpendicular to the pan for practice, begin applying gentle pressure, move away from the pan and lift the tip about ½ inch from the pan. Discontinue pressure and continue moving away—this will break the border off neatly. This is a very simple border and throughout this book you shall see we will use this type of border for many different fill-in decorating procedures.

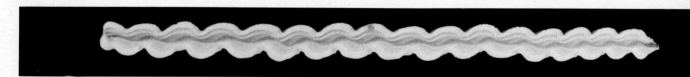

ZIG ZAG BORDER

A No. 87 tip is used for this border, the cone is held at a 45° angle. The tip should be touching the pan at all times. For practice, as you move the tip along, continue a steady side to side motion using an even pressure on the cone at all times. If the border builds up too much, it is because you are using too much pressure. If your icing breaks, you are not applying enough pressure to the cone.

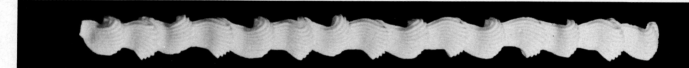

REVERSE SHELL VARIATION

This border is made very much like the reverse shell border and described on the preceding page. A No. 98 tip is used—this is a half moon with a flat shell edge border. As the shell builds up, slightly circle to the left and ease off pressure. The second shell is circled to the right and so on.

SMALL ZIG ZAG

This border is made with a No. 99 tip. The tip lays flat with the two half moon shaped curves of the tip facing up. A small series of back and forth motions gives the effect as illustrated.

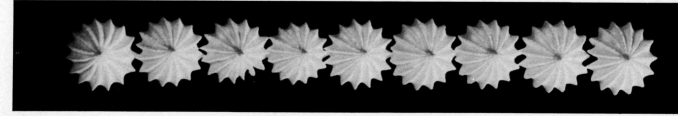

SPECIAL DROP BORDER

A No. 6-B tip is used to make this border. After filling your cone, simply squeeze and relax pressure. These drops may be as large as you desire by squeezing and lifting up on the tip. The more pressure applied, the higher the tip is lifted, the larger each individual drop will be. It is important to keep them uniform, for a smooth finished effect.

LEAF VARIATION

A No. 112 tip is used for this border. After filling the cone, the tip is held at a 45° angle to the surface only tipped on its side at about a 15° angle. This will make one side stand up as illustrated in the picture. As pressure is applied, move the tip along in a continued easy back and forth motion, thus giving the fluted effect.

MEDIUM SHELL VARIATION

A No. 99 tip is used for the medium shell—it is made exactly as the shell border. This is a series of shells connected together in a continuous line, building up on the pressure, lifting the tip up slightly, easing off on the pressure and coming down to a stop.

REVERSE SHELL BORDER

Using a No. 22 tip you will find this border is made the same as the reverse shells explained preceding this border. The No. 22 tip has sharply cut edges and gives a definite design to the border. It also may be used on the upper tier because it is smaller than most reverse shells explained on the preceding pages. Note that when using this No. 22 tip a small amount of pressure is applied. A border about half the size of this may be obtained.

SHELL BORDER VARIATION

The shell border is made with a No. 30 tip. After the shell is completed a No. 104 tip is used. Hold tip at right angles to the border and, by squeezing, lifting up on the tip slightly, and coming down, a separation is made between each shell. This would normally be done in a contrasting color.

SHELL BORDER WITH RUFFLED OUTER EDGE

This border would normally be used at the base of a large cake because of its "bulky" look. A No. 6B tip was used for this border. As the name implies this is a series of shells connected together in a continuous line. The cone is held at a 45° angle to the surface. Begin squeezing, as the shell builds up raise the tip about ½″ —ease off on pressure as you pull down. The shell comes down to a point by stopping all pressure at the end of the shell. A No. 3 tip is used to trim off the outer edge of the shell border and this is done with a series of small back and forth motions as you move from one shell to the other. After this is completed, a single drop is placed in, using the same tip.

DROP FLOWER WITH VARIATIONS

Tip No. 6B is used and the same procedure is followed as in making drop flower border. For the outer trim of each individual drop flower a No. 44 tip is used in a contrasting color. This is a small tip similar to a No. 101 rose tip only it is perfectly flat on each side. The tip must be slanted or held next to the drop border with a continued even pressure squeezing and moving along each individual outside drop flower. The same procedure is followed on the right hand side giving the effect as illustrated. The outer trim is made with a No. 2 tip using a small back and forth zig zag motion, coming in between each drop flower, thus completing your border.

SHELL BORDER WITH FLUTED EDGE

Make a shell as described previously using the No. 195 shell tip. The fluted edge is made using a No. 101 tip and the ruffle on the edge is accomplished by using a slight back and forth motion as you move the tip along the shell. A contrasting color may be used for the fluted edge.

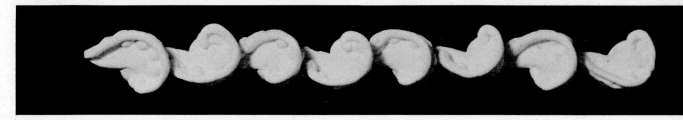

REVERSE BULB BORDER

Use a No. 4P tip and after building the shell up, relax pressure and move in a circular motion slightly to the right. Relax your pressure completely at the bottom. The same procedure is followed for the next reverse except that after the shell is built up, move to the left in a circular motion. The trim is made with a No. 3 tip, circling the reverse shell with small tiny back and forth motions and then overpiped in a smooth singular line as illustrated.

REVERSE BULB BORDER

This border is made exactly as a reverse shell border. A No. 12 tip is used. When the shell builds up, you circle to the right and ease off pressure. The second shell is built up and circled to the left and so on.

ELONGATED REVERSE SHELL

This elongated reverse shell border is made with a No. 30 tip. Each shell is started off first from the left and then to the right, and is used for the edging around the top of a cake.

SMALL ALTERNATING PLUME BORDER

A No. 13 tip was used for the alternating curves. This border may be worked around the side of a cake with a series of up and down motions forming a shallow curving line around the cake. The large and the small plumes are then worked in, alternating from side to side. Beginning at the outside of the plume and squeezing, easing off on pressure and moving in to the curved line. This is a good series to practice on the base of a pan.

MEDIUM SCROLL BORDER

Use a No. 17 star tip for the alternating curves. The pressure must be diminished at the end of each plume.

This entire border may be overpiped with a No. 3 tip in a contrasting color, if so desired.

BULB BORDER WITH "S" SCROLL

The smooth shell effect is obtained using a No. 4P tip with a ⅜ inch opening. The "S" border is put on with a No. 3 tip, using a contrasting color. By taking a close look you will see that the "S" is begun at the front of the shell and passes across the back to the second shell. Notice carefully where the second "S" is started. This border is completed with the "S" scroll. Should you care to go into more detail you may do so as shown. The slight trim on either side of the scroll is done with a No. 2 tip. The small series of back and forth motions, the single drop border at the base of the shell, is made using a No. 3 tip.

UPRIGHT SHELL VARIATION

The upright shell is made with a No. 22 tip. After the entire side of the cake has been circled with an upright shell, a No. 5 tip is used to pipe on the question mark. Starting at the left hand side of the shell, use a steady even pressure and move over the top, around, and down, and finish with a slight curl. This must be done neatly and uniformly for a clean effect, as illustrated.

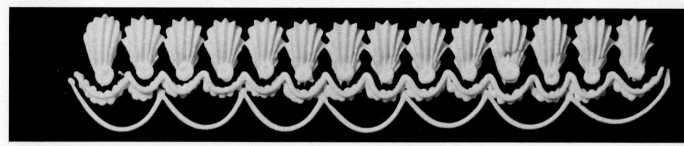

UPRIGHT SHELL VARIATION

The upright shell is made using the No. 22 tip. After circling the side of the cake with the shell a No. 2 tip is used making a series of small back and forth motions. Overpipe this. A single drop border is made using a No. 2 tip and skipping every other shell as illustrated.

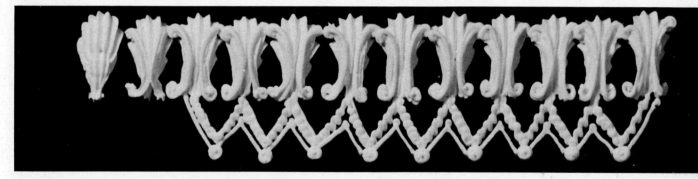

UPRIGHT SHELL WITH SCROLL VARIATION

The shell is made with a No. 22 tip. It is piped on in an upright position on the side of the cake. On either side of the shell 2 half moons are piped on using a No. 13 tip. The half moons are then overpiped using a No. 3 tip. The trim on the base is made with a No. 2 tip.

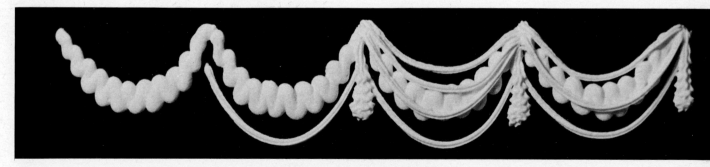

DROPPED GARLAND BORDER

Two tips are used for this border, a No. 58 oval tip and a No. 13 star tip. The first step is to drop a guide line about 2 inches down and 3 inches across, forming a half moon. This guide line should be dropped around the entire cake, using a No. 13 tip. The No. 58 tip is then used to go over your guide line. Move the cone in an up and down motion while following and covering the guide line. After this is completed, 3 strings are dropped over the line as illustrated, starting with the bottom string, and using the No. 13 tip. The tassels between the drops are made with a No. 13 star tip. Starting at the bottom with a heavy pressure and moving in a slight back and forth motion, and easing up on the pressure and moving up.

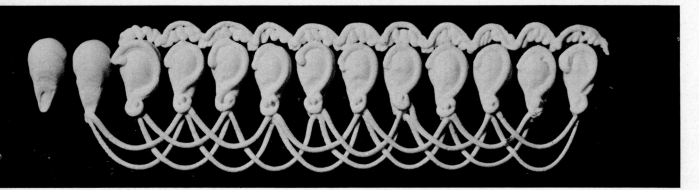

A FEW WORDS ON STRING WORK

We are not covering string or drop borders in this book, as the full series is described and illustrated in our book HOMEMAKER'S ENCYCLOPEDIA OF MODERN CAKE DECORATING. However, we would like to review a few details on string or drop borders. This type of border is frequently referred to as being difficult, while actually string work is easy. The most important thing to remember in string work is to use the proper icing, royal or boiled icing, thinned down to the proper consistency. If your icing is too thin or soft, it will not hold together; too stiff, it will not string out and flow smoothly. A small amount of Karo syrup added to your icing will help it "stretch" or "string out" without breaking. For practice we suggest you work on the side of a cookie pan or similar object that is in an upright position. Each string drops slightly below the other, in a smooth, co-ordinated movement as though it were put on by machine.

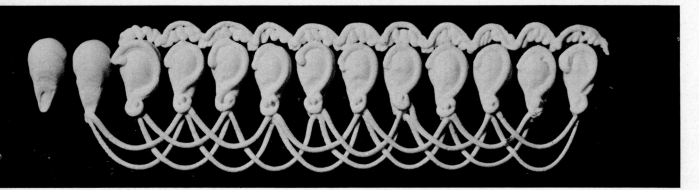

UPRIGHT BULB BORDER WITH DOUBLE DROP

A No. 4P tip is used. A series of shells are made in an upright position. After circling the side of the cake with the upright bulb border, the double drop string work is put on using a No. 3 tip. This is done by first making a single drop border. The single drop is placed on every other bulb. After this is completed repeat the border again but this time let each drop fall about ¼ inch below the first. This gives the drop border the complicated interwoven look. A "question mark" is then piped over each bulb with a No. 3 tip with a smooth continuous motion starting at the top, circling around and curving back to the right, at the bottom of the bulb. The trim over the top of the bulb border is a series of small back and forth motions. After this is completed it is overpiped with a single string using a No. 3 tip. This is a rather complicated looking border, but when broken down into steps it is quite simple to make and certainly enhances the overall beauty of a decorated cake.

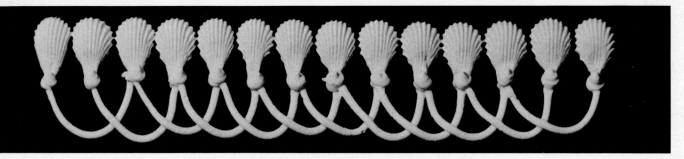

UPRIGHT SHELL WITH SINGLE DROP

A border such as this would normally be used on the side of the top tier of a wedding cake. The shell is made with a No. 172 tip—starting on the side on the top of the cake, squeeze out a shell, ease off on the pressure and move down. Continue this procedure until the entire cake is circled. A No. 5 tip is used for the drop border skipping every other shell, as illustrated. After the drop border is completed a small dot may be piped on the base of each shell, giving a neatly finished effect.

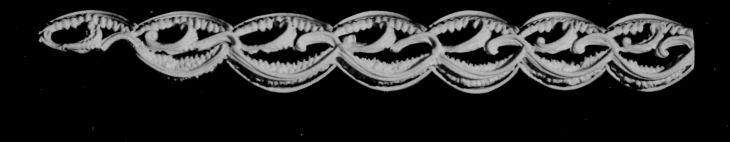

REVERSED SCROLL EDGING BORDER

The reversed scroll is first outlined with a No. 3 tube as shown in the first step. After the outline is completed a No. 16 star tube is used to build up the scroll. The scroll is overpiped with a No. 3 tube. The bottom portion of the border is very similar to a draped garland. This is also done with a No. 16 star tube starting with very light pressure, building the pressure up, and then easing off. With the use of the star tube a single drop is placed over the draped garland. Upon completion, another single drop is placed on top of the first drop using a No. 3 tube. With the use of the same tube another drop is placed on below that completing the bottom of the border. The top of the border is finished off with a No. 3 tube using a series of back and forth motions and then overpiped using the same tube.

DRAPED SCROLL BORDER

This border is done on the edge of the cake. The scroll is the heaviest part of the border and is built up with a No. 16 star tube, as shown in the first step. The next step is to overpipe this using the same tube. After it is completed a No. 3 tube is used and you again overpipe directly on top of your first overpiping. The border is finished off at the top and also the bottom in the same manner using a No. 3 tube in a series of back and forth motions finishing with a double drop border.

CURVED SCROLL BORDER

This border is worked on the side and top of the cake. A No. 16 star tube is used to make the curved scroll which is placed directly on the edge of the cake, as shown in the first step. This curved scroll is then overpiped with the same tube. After completing that a No. 3 tube is used to overpipe this curved scroll again. The draped garland directly under the curved scroll is made with a No. 16 star tube. The top of the border which goes around the top of the cake is completed with a No. 3 tube in a series of small back and forth motions and then, using the same tube. the curved line beyond that, is piped on completing the border.

SEGREGATED SCROLL BASE BORDER

By following the picture or the steps very closely, this border is almost self explanatory. To build the scroll up as shown in Step 1, a No. 16 star tube is used. This is sort of an elongated S. The scroll is started off with a very easy pressure using a slight back and forth movement of the tube. The pressure is built up and then eased off again as you finish the scroll. After completing this around the entire cake, the same tube is used for the overpiping of the scroll, shown in Step 2. The next step is to over-pipe on top of this again, with the use of a No. 3 tube. The top of the border is finished off with a No. 3 tube using a series of back and forth motions. After this is completed the single line is piped on using the same tube. The bottom part of the border is made with the same No. 3 tube. Make a series of back and forth motions starting with very easy pressure and then getting a little heavier and then easing off pressure again when you come to the end of the curved line. This border is worked on the base of the cake.

DROPPED GARLAND BORDER

Another base border. Step No. 1 is made with a No. 16 star tube. Starting off with very easy pressure, move the tube in a back and forth motion, building up in the center and then ease off as you come to the end of the garland. After completing this, the No. 16 tube is used for the single drop around the bottom of the garland. A No. 3 tube is used to make another drop directly on top of the first one. The top of the border is completed with two small drops and then a small bow connecting the drops as shown in the above border. The bottom of the border is finished off with a No. 3 tube with a series of small back and forth motions. After this is completed, a No. 67 tube is used and a leaf is piped underneath each section where the border meets.

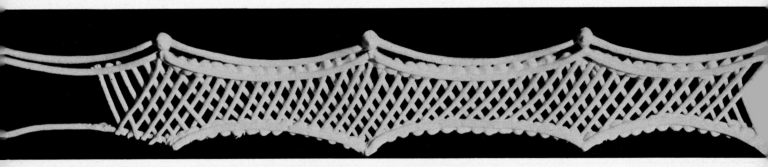

LATTICE SCALLOP BORDER

This border is normally worked in bridging the first and second tier of a wedding cake. It is a very beautiful and complicated border but when broken down into steps, it becomes simple to make. The outline is made on the cake using a No. 3 tube. Each section of this border is approximately 2½ inches long. The outline is then bridged across with lattice work. The lattice work should be kept at a 45 degree angle. After the lattice work is completed the No. 3 tube is used to go over or cover up the rough edges where a lattice meets the outline. The next step is to run a single line over the entire bottom portion of the lattice. The top of the border is completed in the same manner and one more single drop is placed directly above the lattice with a dot connecting each section.

RUFFLED GARLAND BORDER

The garland is first piped on the side of the cake using a No. 30 star tube. This garland is piped on in the same manner as described for Full Garland border. The ruffle is then piped on with the use of a No. 104 tube. After completing this, a single drop border is placed over it, using a No. 16 tube. Two single drops are placed beneath the garland border using the No. 3 tube. The curved scrolls on the top of the cake are worked in using the No. 16 star tube. The entire top of the border is then overpiped using a No. 3 tube.

GARLAND BORDER WITH RUFFLE TRIM

The garland is piped on with a No. 16 star tube. After it is completed, the ruffle trim is piped on using the No. 104 tube. This is done at the top and bottom of the garland. Two small curved lines are then piped on the top of the garland using the No. 16 star tube. A single drop border is then worked in underneath the small curves. A No. 3 tube is used to overpipe these lines. Where the border connects a No. 67 leaf tube is used to make the leaves. The single drop border is then placed under the ruffle trim.

FLUTED CRESCENT BORDER

This border is worked around the top of a cake. The guide lines are first piped on using the No. 3 tube. Each crescent is approximately 2 inches long. After the guide line is complete, a No. 104 tube is used for the fluted edge. The heavy end of the tube touches the cake, the small end stands out. Using a steady pressure in a series of back and forth motions, the fluted edge is completed.

The edge is then overpiped with a No. 3 tube. The bottom portion of the border is made with a No. 3 tube using a series of back and forth motions. The double string is dropped over this completing the bottom section. The series of curved lines around the top of the border is made with a No. 3 tube.

REVERSED "S" FLUTE BORDER

The reversed S is piped on using the No. 16 star tip. This border is piped directly on the edge of the cake. The No. 104 tip is used to make a fluted edge. After the fluted edge is completed, the underside of the border is trimmed with a No. 16 star tip and overpiped with a No. 3 tip.

STAR BORDER WITH STRING WORK

A No. 30 star tube is used to make the stars or points. These must be placed on the top of the cake. After completing this, No. 16 is used to work around the base of each star. The double drop border is then put on, using a No. 3 tube as explained under string work. Another double drop is then dropped around the base of the border.

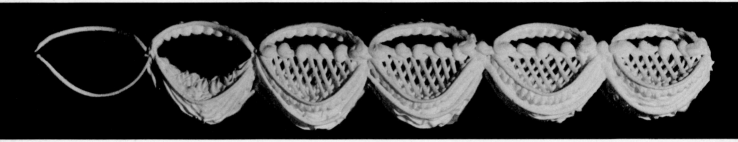

LATTICE GARLAND BORDER

The outline is made with a No. 3 tube. The garland was put on using a No. 30 tube as explained previously. The lattice work is put on at a 45 degree angle using a No. 3 tube. Using the same No. 3 tube, two strings are then dropped under the lattice work. The top of the border is finished off with a No. 3 tube and the edge of the cake is covered with a reverse shell using the No. 3 tube.

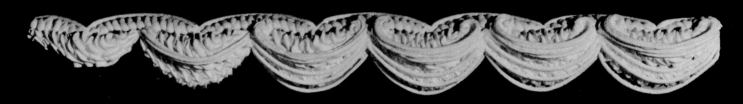

DRAPED GARLAND AND SCROLL BORDER

No. 16 star tube is used for the garland. The garland is then bordered underneath with the use of the small star tube. A single drop is placed under the garland with a No. 16 tube. This is overpiped with a No. 3 tube and a series of three strings are then piped below this. The top of the border is self explanatory.

GARLAND VARIATIONS

This is another border that is worked around the top edging of the cake, and is done in exactly the same way as the above border. The only difference with this border is that the C scroll has not been piped on. By studying these borders very closely and observing the steps in the pictures, you will be able to follow them after a few practice trys. Keep your borders uniform and neat. The more practice and concentration given to these borders, the finer your work will become.

REVERSE SHELL BORDER

Just as the name implies, this is a series of reverse shells connected together in a continuous line. The tip used for this border is a large tip called the No. 7B tip. This border would normally be used at the base of a wedding cake or the bottom tier of your cake. Hold the cone at a 45° angle to the cake surface and begin squeezing. As the shell builds up raise the tip about ½ inch—then ease off on your pressure as you come down or back to the base, circling first to the left and then building up and easing off and circling to the right, thus giving the reversed effect.

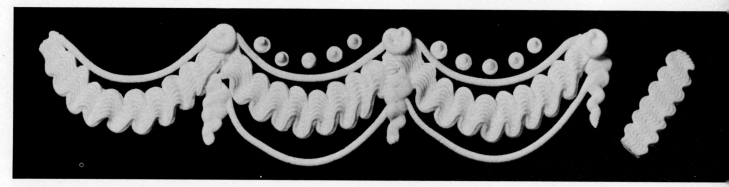

GARLAND VARIATION

First, drop a guide line around the cake about 2 to 3 inches in width and 1½ inches down—go over this guide line with a No. 48 tip. The No. 48 tip is a flat edged type tip much like a No. 104, which most of you are familiar with, except that it has many little teeth in the end. Using a uniform pressure, move the tip in an up and down motion, as you follow along your drop guide line. A No. 5 tip is used for the drop above each fluted edge and also for the drop below. The five dots in each section of border are also placed on with the use of a No. 5 tip. The leaf type effect where each border connects is made with the No. 48 tip, starting at the top, squeezing heavy and moving down with a side to side motion, easing off and relaxing pressure, thus bringing this leaf type effect to a point.

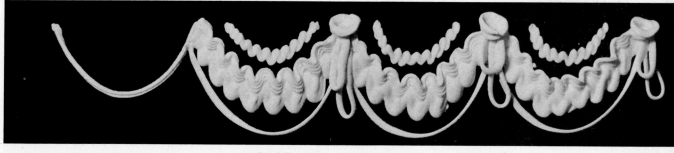

GARLAND VARIATION

Using a No. 55 tip, a guide line is dropped around the entire cake as shown in step 1. This tip has an oval type opening and gives the dropped line a flat appearance. The garland effect is made with a No. 62 tip. Using an even pressure on the cone, move the tip in an up and down motion on the guide line. After this is completed the border is then finished off with the No. 55 tip using a single drop under each garland. Two small drop lines are worked between each crescent and finished off at the top with a series of circular motions giving a bell appearance. The upper portion of the garland is then filled in with a series of small back and forth motions, using the same No. 55 tip. We suggest that you practice the fluted edge and most of these borders shown here on the side of an upright pan. After a few practice attempts you will be ready to put this border on your cake.

A FINAL WORD ON BORDERS

When putting a shell, or similar border around the top edge of a cake, do not work your border directly on top of the cake—but work it slightly to the side, say at about a 15 degree angle. This will cover up the edge of the cake.

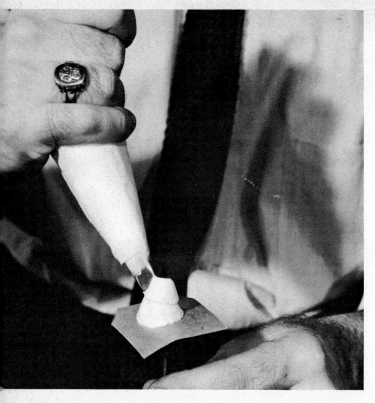

To construct the base of the rose, the cone is held in the right hand with the small end of the tube pointing up and toward the center of the nail. Continue squeezing the cone and turning the nail until you have a fairly wide base. Another dome is then started directly on top of the first dome.

This is the proper position and angle of the tube when making the three small petals around the top portion of the dome which completes the bud.

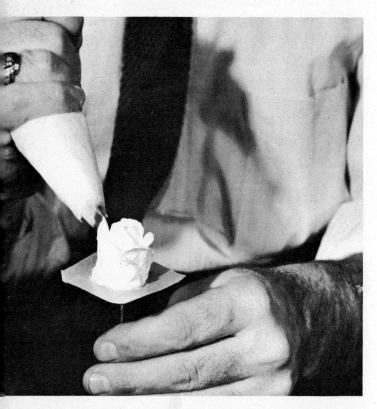

This is the position of the tube when making the second five petals directly under the bud. The petals stand out slightly. To do this the tube must stand out slightly as illustrated.

The last row of petals must stand out. This is accomplished by simply turning the tube out more to the side.

AMERICAN BEAUTY ROSE

As the name implies this is truly an American Beauty and when properly made the rose is the loveliest flower made with the tube. Make this flower with a No. 124 rose tube that has a straight edge and permits control of the "roll" at the petal's edge. Buttercream, royal or boiled icing may be used. Be sure it is stiff enough so that the petals stand up. Strip the cone by using a spatula-knife and pink icing. Start the strips at the base of the tube at the wide opening. Continue it up through the cone. Fill the remainder of the cone with white icing. This gives you a natural two-tone rose effect. Stick a small piece of waxed paper on the head of nail. After the flower is completed slide the paper off the nail onto a pan. With this method as many flowers as desired may be made using one nail.

The first step is to construct the base with a small dome of icing about 1½ inches high. The nail should be turned in a counter clockwise motion. The cone is held in the right hand with the small end of the tube pointing up and slightly toward the center of the nail. Start squeezing the cone and turning the nail. Continue squeezing and turning until you have a fairly wide base. Another dome is then started directly on top of the first dome. Three small petals are then placed around the top part of the dome which completes the bud or top portion of the rose. The next five petals are placed on slightly under the bud and stand out a little more than the petals of the bud. In placing these petals make sure to overlap each one slightly. To complete the last row start at the very bottom of the base. Squeezing while you turn the nail in a co-ordinated motion, lift the tube slightly and then return to the bottom of the base. Continue the petals all the way around the bottom of the dome completing the flower. Here are some common mistakes in making the American Beauty Rose. First: Making the rose too flat. This results when the dome or base of the petals is not high enough or when each row of petals is not started below the preceding row. Second: The petals are too tight. This is caused by holding the tube in toward the dome. Third: Petals are flat looking, caused by holding the tube to the side or away from the dome or base. Fourth: Wavy petals. Squeezing the bag too heavily or turning the nail too slowly will result in this. It is evident why the rose is a difficult flower to execute properly. Have patience and practice it diligently.

FAIRYLAND CASTLE CAKE

A real fairyland castle cake absolutely out of this world, icing, cake and silver candy balls, standing on a hill of coconut. Yum, yum, yum! Now don't let it scare you, for the steps are quite simple. Mother and daughter can work on this project together. This can be the biggest surprise of your little guy's life. The cake we use is baked in our square tier cake pan set. The base is made of two 9″ layers, the second tier, two 6″ layers, and the last tier two 4″ layers cut out and formed into a circle. After the cake is iced, the tall towers on each corner of the cake are made from 2½″ in diameter cylinders. These may be made in cardboard or from cans and should be approximately 5″ high. They are iced and placed into each corner of the base. The cylinder or tower in the center of the cake is three inches high. Five cardboard cones are made as illustrated and stapled together forming the roof of the towers. Before the cake is placed on a base, a moat may be drawn around and brushed with blue thinned down royal icing. The two layer 9″ cake is decorated first. We used our light fluffy boiled icing made with a meringue powder. A No. 7 tip is used filled with white icing, starting at the base of the cake, a row of bulbs or white balls are formed by squeezing and relaxing pressure. The next row is started immediately above the first and this is continued until the

entire wall is completed. The second and third tier are formed in the same manner working from the base all the way around and then moving up to the next row. It is a simple matter of filling in the entire wall section with white balls of icing. Before placing the towers on each corner, we suggest that you work on each individual tower starting at the base using a No. 6 tip. The cone that fits over the tower may be iced with a thinned down royal icing. While the icing is still moist, sprinkle silver dragees over the tower or cone. Then place the gaily colored contrasting dragees around the cone to give the tower a fantasia effect. After the five towers are decorated, they are then placed into position on the corners as illustrated. Four small cones are placed on each corner of the six inch cake and a large silver dragee is used to top each tower. At the top of each tier, forming the wall, a white ball of icing is spaced at half inch intervals and topped off with a large silver dragee. The flags are made from a stiff cardboard and iced with gaily colored royal icing. After the flags are dried they are stuck to the flag pole and placed above the towers. The draw bridge is made in cardboard and iced with royal icing. Coconut is used for the grass and colored with delicate green. This is done by putting a small amount of diluted paste color into the coconut and rubbing it between the palms of the hand.

BABY SHOWER CAKE or
TODDLERS FIRST BIRTHDAY CAKE

Whatever may be the occasion, this is certain to please. Seven 4½"x4½" cake squares are iced in the gay colors as illustrated. Two layer 10" cake is then iced in white icing and placed on top of the seven squares. The blocks are trimmed with a reverse shell using the No. 17 star tip. A special No. 6B tip is used to trim off the base of the 10" cake. The reverse shell is made with a No. 22 tip circling the top of the cake. The brightly colored animals on the sides of the blocks are made from our animal mold set using the sugar mold method. The numbers and A B C's are also made with our sugar mold. The two booties on top are made again with the sugar mold using our bootie molds and then covered in royal icing with a No. 22 tip. This knitting effect is obtained by simple squeezing and relaxing pressure using a fill-in method covering the entire bootie. The ruffle around the top of each bootie is made with the No. 101 rose tip. The large roses circling the booties are made with the No. 124 rose tip.

CIRCUS TRAIN CAKE

An ideal centerpiece for a child's party. Each of the train cakes were made the following way. The base of each train car was made using a 4x6″ cake trimmed in any desirable colored icing using a No. 47 tip. It was placed on a 2x3″ square block to lift it up slightly from the surface. The wheels were made with cookies iced in white icing and trimmed in red using a No. 13 tip. The top of the circus train cake was made of a sheet of ½″ styrofoam cut 4x6″ in length. The colorful striped straws are placed at about 1″ above the top of the styrofoam. Straight pins were used to push through

the straws and into the styrofoam to hold them in their proper position. The straws were then cut to their desired length and placed on the animal train cake. All of the animals in the train are made from the sugar mold method using our No. 301 animal set. The three colorful decorated cakes were placed on a base covered with green coconut and trimmed in large silver dragees. The brilliantly colored clowns were placed between the cars of the circus cake which gives the youngsters the feeling that it's time for the next act to begin so let's get on with the circus.

This, we feel, is somewhat unusual in the cake decorating field. Almost anything that you may imagine can be created, in frosting, cake, and ribbons. This colorful display most assuredly will prove our point.

Our finished product stood 24″ high. The balloon was baked off in two sections using a 12″ mixing bowl for the mold. The same idea can be carried out on a little smaller basis by using a 9 or 10″ mixing bowl and assembling the cake in the following manner: Using a 14″ wooden base, a ¼″ pipe was attached to two crow's feet, approximately 3″ in diameter. The crow's feet were screwed into the wooden base, and a heavy pie plate which was used to set the cake on and was attached to the top of the pipe by four metal screws and bolts. After the two half cakes were baked and cooled they were then iced and put together forming the balloon. A few long sticks or dowel rods were driven through the two sections to hold them together. After the cake was iced, a smooth finished surface was obtained by dipping a brush into warm water and brushing the boiled icing. The basket for the balloon was made of styrofoam using six 1″ circles, placed one on top of another, cutting out the center and cutting in half and placing the half sections together, forming the basket around the pipe. The basket was woven with a No. 46 and No. 46° tips. It would not be necessary to weave your basket, you may work a border using the No. 46 tip in an up and down motion circling your basket with 10 different rows and giving almost the same effect. The pipe was iced in royal icing and covered with ribbon. The ribbons which simulate the attachment to the basket and balloon were placed on in the following manner: Using a string we measured the distance from the top of the basket over the top of the balloon back around to the top of the basket. Five ½″ wide ribbons using various gay colors were cut out to this length and placed over the top of the balloon and draped down to either side thus forming the ten strands as shown. These were connected to the decorated styrofoam base with the use of straight pins.

The small silver net bags were filled with large candy dragees simulating the type bags that are dropped from balloons to increase altitude in flight. A few of the large dragees were placed around the green base of icing. The small balloon border on the trimming of the wooden base was made with the No. 12 tip using the many colors as illustrated. The finely detailed clown was 7½″ high, distinctive in detail with his oversized bow tie, floppy shoes, and flowing coat. Everyone raved about this new creation. We never did find out how good it was to eat because no one wanted to cut it.

INTRODUCTION TO SUGAR MOLD METHOD

We shall describe and illustrate the types of sugar molding used with variations of Wilton sugar molds.

Blend mix and sugar together using a large spoon, or the best way to mix them thoroughly is to rub the sugar and paste between the palms of the hands and through the fingers until it is worked evenly throughout the granulated sugar.

In humid climates the mold should be dusted before mixture is inserted. To accomplish this place 4 table-spoons of cornstarch in a thin cloth and tie to form a bag. Dust mold lightly with this bag.

Pack mixture solidly into mold and scrape off excess with a knife.

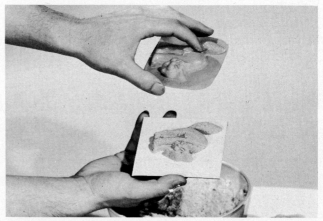

Place pre-cut cardboard square over mold and turn gently upside down as illustrated. Sugar may be swiftly dried, by placing in preheated oven (200°) for 5 minutes or placing in direct sunlight.

THE SUGAR MOLD METHOD

There are three methods in preparing the sugar mix to be used in the sugar mold method. The first is with sugar and water, the second using sugar and egg white, the third is with sugar, meringue powder and water.

SUGAR WATER RECIPE

3 teaspoons water
2 cups sugar
Sugar and water is mixed together until the moisture is distributed evenly throughout the sugar. This may be done with a mixer at slow speed, worked in with a spoon, or rubbed between the hands to insure a more thorough distribution. This recipe would normally be used to make tiny sugar molds for a tea or similar occasion.

SUGAR AND EGG WHITE RECIPE

2½ lbs. granulated sugar
1 egg white
Sugar and egg white is mixed until the egg white is worked evenly throughout the sugar. Using a sticky substance such as egg white, the sugar mold becomes much harder and will stand up better in humid climate.

SUGAR, MERINGUE POWDER AND WATER RECIPE

3 teaspoons meringue powder
3 teaspoons warm water
2 cups granulated sugar
Mix water and meringue powder until thoroughly dissolved. Add sugar and mix thoroughly to insure even distribution of all ingredients. The meringue powder acts much like the egg white and gives the sugar a stronger body after the mold hardens. This recipe will stand up better in humid climates.

Any type of mold may be used for the sugar mold method. The Wiltons have developed a series of sugar mold sets designed especially for the many variations of cake decorating we believe the average housewife would be interested in.

WILTON SUGAR MOLD SETS

WRITING SET—words, phrases, letters and numerals for making any message.

CUB SCOUT AND BOY SCOUT EMBLEMS
6 Inch Dia.

BROWNIE AND GIRL SCOUT EMBLEMS
6 Inch Dia.

ANIMAL SET—8 favorite animal molds specially loved by children.

MASONIC AND EASTERN STAR EMBLEMS
6 Inch Dia.

KNIGHTS OF COLUMBUS AND LIONS INTERNATIONAL. 6 Inch Dia.

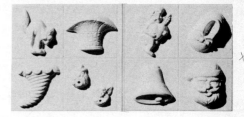

HOLIDAY SET—9 different molds for favorite holidays.

VARIETY SUGAR MOLDING SET—Large Slippers, Good Luck Horseshoe, Book and Cross.

CHRISTMAS ORNAMENT SET—9 molds that will add to the gayety of the season.

MOTHER GOOSE SET—8 favorite characters beloved by everyone.

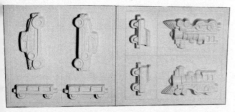

OLD TIME TRAIN & CAR—This mold has a right and left half that can be placed together with royal icing to make a complete unit.

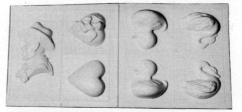

NEW ASSORTMENT — This variety mold also has right and left halfs that can be placed together. Popular requested swan, duck, cupid heart and cowboy.

FLOWER SET—37 flower, leaf and bud molds...including 4 birds.

EASTER EGG MOLDS — Three two-piece Easter Egg Molds — made from heavy transparent plastic—perfect for chocolate or sugar molding.

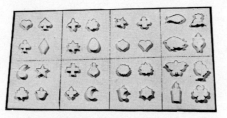

SUGAR CUBE MOLDING SET—32 new and unusual designs for sugar cube molding. Just perfect for cake decorating or may be served during coffee or tea.

SPECIAL OCCASION SET—32 different molds for all events.

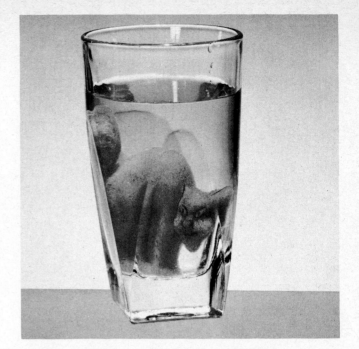

MULTICOLORING   MULTICOLORING SUGAR FOR PARTY DRINK

Different colors can be used in one mold by mixing separate batches and applying the colors in the mold where desired. Faces and figures can be artfully colored by inserting the desired shades in the mold with a toothpick or other sharp implement, then packing the remainder of the mold with bulk mix.

Before putting your sugar into the molds dust the inside of the mold with cornstarch. After dusting the mold with cornstarch the sugar mixture is placed into the mold as illustrated.

After the sugar is packed down and is smoothed on the surface, drop the mold out on a sheet of waxed paper as illustrated. Any number of sugar forms may be made using the one mold. The sugar mold is then allowed to dry for approximately two hours. The air will harden the outside of the sugar mold. The mold is lifted up and the inside is hollowed out as illustrated. The sugar from the inside of the mold will still be soft and moist and may be used for more sugar molds. The longer the sugar mold dries, the thicker the sugar form will be.

SUGAR MOLD
FOR TEA TIME
Just another example
of the many uses of the
Wilton sugar molds.

BASKET TOP CAKE

"A tisket, a tasket, a green and yellow basket." The border is made in yellow icing using the No. 46 tip with a slight side to side motion. The basket, flowers and leaves are all made with the sugar mold method. After drying, they are placed on the cake top. The stems and handle of the basket are made in green icing using the No. 3 tip. The basket is tied with a yellow bow using the No. 104 tip.

CROSS CAKE TOP

This is an 8″ cake decorated with a shell bulb border using the No. 10 tip. The shell is piped on in a pale blue icing. The S scroll worked over the shell was made with a No. 5 tip in white icing. The crosses are made in pale blue. The center large cross is made of two colors. The white is placed in the mold first and then a pale blue sugar was packed on top of the cross giving it a two tone effect.

GRADUATION CAKE

This cake is iced in white. The reverse shell border is made with the No. 4B tip. The three diplomas are made of white sugar and the small bows tying the diploma are yellow. The open book is made with a two tone effect by packing white sugar into the book mold, and then filling the remainder of the mold with bright yellow. Yale—1970 is piped on with No. 3 tip using brown colored icing.

GOOD LUCK CAKE

This is an 8″ cake. The drop flower border is made with the No. 195 tip in green icing. By using a simple squeeze and stop pressure on each drop flower, a uniform design is obtained. The horseshoe is dropped out using the sugar mold method in yellow sugar. Three small horseshoes are then worked around the cake as illustrated. All molds shown in this picture are from the Wilton sugar molds.

47

ANNIVERSARY CAKE

The border is made with the No. 88 tip using pale blue icing. The three pale blue bells are dropped from the Wilton sugar mold and are tied in pale blue icing, using the No. 88 tip. "First Anniversary" is written in a deep blue icing with the No. 2 tip.

YELLOW JONQUIL CAKE

This is a 9″ Angel Food Cake iced with a white boiled icing. The yellow jonquils are made by using the Wilton sugar molds and were the only decoration placed on this cake.

HALLOWEEN CAKE

The border on this cake is made in a bright yellow icing using the No. 172 tip. The outside trim of the border is made with white icing and a No. 44 tip. The cat, moon, pumpkins were made with the sugar mold method in appropriate colors, and stalks of corn made using the No. 4 tip.

CORNUCOPIA CAKE

The cake is iced in white. The reverse shell is made with the No. 22 tip using a delicate violet shade. The cornucopia and grapes are made with the sugar mold method. The vines are piped on the cake with a No. 3 tip.

EASTER BASKET

The cake was iced in white icing. The stucco effect was obtained by placing the flat edge of the spatula against the icing and pulling away. A series of these strokes will create this stucco effect. The upper portion of the cake border was trimmed with a No. 104 tip. The Easter eggs were made with the sugar mold method in pale green, yellow, blue and violet. The basket was made of yellow sugar and trimmed in green icing using the No. 3 tip.

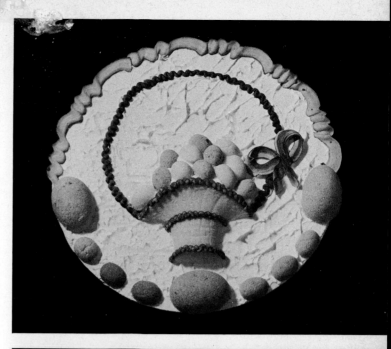

EASTER CAKE

The entire cake was decorated, using the sugar mold method. The Easter eggs were made using alternating colors of pale yellow, blue, green, violet and pink. The two eggs in the center were hollowed out and were made of green sugar. The small chicks hopping across the cake were in yellow sugar. All molds illustrated were from the Wilton sugar molds.

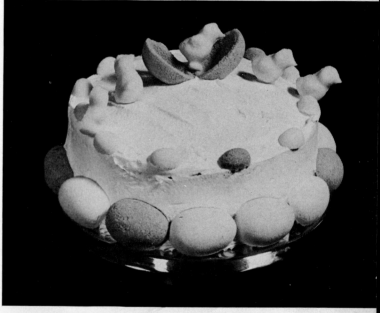

DECORATED EASTER EGG MOLD FACES

The Easter eggs are made using the sugar mold method. They are hollow, and after drying the two sections are stuck together with royal icing. The mold used is our small Easter egg mold which is 3″x2″. A few variations with the face, hat and hair will give the following results, which we think are quite cute conversation pieces. The collar or the base for the Easter egg mold is done in royal icing with a No. 104 tip and the finished product may then be sprinkled with silver glitter.

The base to stand the egg on is molded in a small dish or egg cup using sugar mold method or a cardboard collar can be made and decorated.

CHRISTMAS TREE ORNAMENTS

We featured these lovely Christmas Tree Ornaments in National Magazines and received so many nice letters about them, we thought you'd like to know how to make them too. So many people made them to hang on their Christmas trees or to sell at Church, club and scouting fund raising events. They are extremely easy to make using the sugar mold recipe on page 44. Your entire family can join in on the fun. Just follow these simple steps....

Dry molds at room temperature for 40 minutes. To speed drying place them in a preheated 200° oven for 5 minutes. Hold each one in your hand and scoop out inside sugar very gently with a spoon. Shell should be about ¼″ thick.

Paste a loop of ribbon to top inside edge of mold with icing (if ornament is to hang) and outline the entire edge of the mold with a generous coating of icing. Then press halves together gently.

Decorate by applying a dot or a line or a circle of icing to the sugar ornament. While the icing is still damp, attach dragees (do this with tweezers; it's easier) and sprinkle the damp icing with glitter.

You can color these ornaments using the methods noted on page 46. Also, add extra beauty by piping hard dry icings on in decorative forms. Glitter or colorful tiny decorating candy may be sprinkled on the damp icing before it becomes dry.

FILL-IN METHOD OF FIGURE PIPING

The Wiltons have devised this method of figure piping making it possible for the beginner to pipe almost any type of figure. In this chapter we have designed twenty variations of cake tops, each drawn out and illustrated in detail. A sheet of waxed paper may be placed over the drawing, and using royal icing the drawings may be filled in as one would fill in with a crayola, except the icing will take height and depth. After the royal icing dries, it may be peeled off the waxed paper and placed on a cake top.

HALLOWEEN   EASTER

CHRISTMAS   THANKSGIVING

CHILD'S BIRTHDAY CAKE

Cake is iced in white. Using a No. 7 tip, the jolly little duck is piped in with the fill in method in yellow and features are drawn in with a No. 2 tip, using brown icing. Pale pink roses are made with the No. 104 tip and the leaves are made with a No. 67 leaf tip. "Happy Birthday" is printed in with red icing, using a No. 4 tip.

FISHERMAN BIRTHDAY

Ice upper ⅓ of the cake in light blue, bottom ⅔ in a darker greenish blue. Outline the land in brown and fill in the boat and man using brown, yellow, and pink.

The jumping fish are piped on in orange and the "Happy Birthday" in bright yellow. Use a No. 6 tip for fill in, and a No. 3 tip to write.

HAPPY BIRTHDAY *Jackie*

ROCKET TO THE MOON

Ice cake in desired color. Make rocket in blue and red. Using No. 7 tip, fill in cowboy in light blue and yellow, hat in brown. "Happy Birthday" is written in bright red, with a No. 3 tip.

BON VOYAGE

Cake may be iced in any desired color. "Mayflower" is piped on using the fill in method over waxed paper. A brown royal icing for the "Mayflower" and pink and white icing for the sails. After drying they are placed on the cake and "Bon Voyage" may be written in chocolate. A No. 2 and No. 5 tip is used for the fill in method.

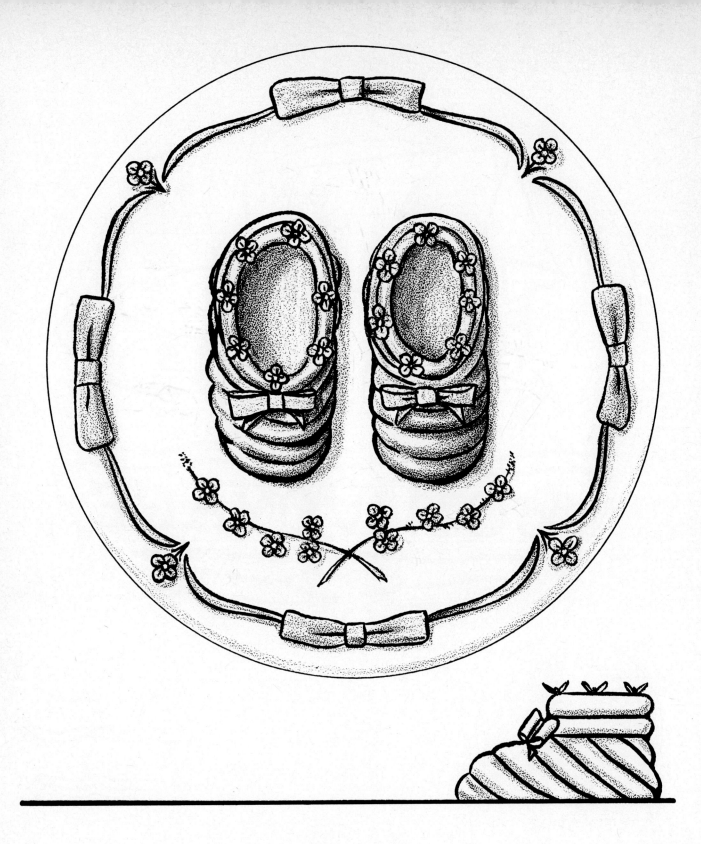

BABY BOOTIES

Baby booties may be made with the sugar mold method using the Wilton Sugar Mold. After the bootie dries, it may be over-piped with a No. 8 tip as illustrated. The border around the outside of the cake is done in a pale pink icing, using a No. 101 tip. Tiny drop flowers and a vine are worked in at the toe of the booties.

FLOWER BASKET

Cake is iced with white icing. The basket is piped in with a No. 8 tip in brown. Shell border around the top and bottom of the basket is in yellow and made with a No. 19 tip. The flowers are made ahead of time in royal icing, and placed on as illustrated. A small vine and tiny blue flowers are worked in around the outside of the cake to simulate a border. Bow is tied with a yellow bow using tip No. 103.

MOTHER'S DAY CAKE

The initial and writing is done in rose colored icing. The carnations are made with a No. 104 tip in pale pink icing and the stems are made with a No. 3 tip in green icing.

STYROFOAM CANOPY DESIGN WITH STEPS

The complete styrofoam backdrop, cross and steps were made of ½″ styrofoam. The back of the arch stood 10″ high and the steps were 14″ wide. After the sections were placed together using straight pins to fasten the sections, the entire styrofoam piece was iced with a thinned down royal icing. The lattice design over the arch of the styrofoam was made with a No. 3 tip for the lattice work and trimmed with a No. 16 tip to give the lattice sections strength. After the pieces hardened they were stuck into position. The bride, groom, and flower girls are all available from our supply catalog. Silver glitter was sprinkled around the steps, doorway and top piece, to give the centerpiece a decorative effect.

STYROFOAM FLOAT

For this gaily adorned styrofoam float, we did not use a pattern. The entire float was cut out of ½″ styrofoam and assembled using straight pins to connect the various sections together. The base of the float was then painted with a thinned down royal icing. The float was trimmed with a No. 16 tip and No. 3 dragees placed on the border. The upper section of the float was trimmed with pink rosebuds and sprinkled with silver glitter. The dolls riding the float seem to be having a merry time. The two swans were made of gumpaste and were tied to the float with ribbon. This festive piece certainly attracted a lot of attention.

GIFT BOX

The cake is iced in a white icing. Ribbon is tied around the cake in a pale pink icing using a No. 127 tip as illustrated. The bow is made with a No. 104 tip. The candle is made with a No. 5 tip in a pale pink icing.

MERRY CHRISTMAS

Ice cake in white. Using brown or chocolate, draw in window design and church. Branches are in green.

Bells may be made in pink, red or green. Small Christmas trees are made in green using the No. 1 tip.

SANTA CLAUS

Cake is iced in pink. Santa is made in red, white, and pink. The fern is made with a No. 2 tip in green and the pine cone is made with a No. 2 tip in brown. Merry Christmas is printed in bright red.

MERRY CHRISTMAS CANDLE

The candle is made using the fill in method. A sheet of waxed paper is placed over the picture and the candle is filled in with red royal icing using a No. 5 tip. The candle may be smoothed out using a brush dipped in water. The melted wax on the top is filled in with No. 3 tip. The candle is placed on the cake and the green fern is put in with a No. 1 tip. The pine cones are made with a No. 1 tip in brown. The outer edge is trimmed in deep green with a red holly berry. The bow on the candle is tied with a No. 101 tip.

MERRY CHRISTMAS

Half of a cake is iced in pale blue icing. The lower half in white to simulate the snow. The Church is piped out with the fill in method using a No. 4 tip with pink, yellow or white icing for the snow. "Merry Christmas" is printed in red. The green foliage for the trees is piped on with a No. 67 leaf tip in green icing.

NEW YEAR CLOCK

Ice this cake in white. The clock face and design is filled in with chocolate or brown icing. The two bells on either side are filled in with red and green icing using a No. 3 tip. "Happy New Year" is printed in red using a No. 3 tip.

HAPPY NEW YEAR

With the No. 6 tip, this entire cake may be made using the fill in method. A sheet of waxed paper is placed over the drawing. The glass is filled in with yellow. The new year baby is in pink with a bright yellow diaper. The hat is done in black. The year is filled in with a bright yellow and the champagne bubbles are made with a No. 2 tip in bright pink, yellow and blue dots.

WASHINGTON'S BIRTHDAY CAKE

Ice cake in white. Make hatchet and branches in brown icing and No. 5 tip. Red piping jelly is used for the cherries. Green piping jelly for the leaves in a No. 65 tip.

RABBIT AND CHICKS

Cake is iced in white icing. Rabbit is piped out with the fill in method using a No. 7 tip and pale pink icing. Carrot is piped on with a No. 5 tip in orange. The two chicks are piped on using the fill in method in yellow icing with a No. 7 tip. After drying they are placed on the cake as illustrated. The grass is made with a No. 3 tip using a series of lines to simulate a grass design.

HALLOWEEN CAKE

Upper portion of the cake is iced in orange. Lower portion is iced in brown. The cat is made using the fill in method on waxed paper in black icing and a No. 7 tip. The pumpkin is made with the fill in method using a No. 8 tip in bright orange. The leaves are piped on in green using a No. 67 leaf tip. A border is worked around the outside of the cake in yellow icing, using a No. 8 tip.

THANKSGIVING CAKE

Ice cake in orange icing. A sheet of waxed paper may be placed over the drawing and filled in the following manner: A No. 3 tip is used to fill in the faces of the boy and girl. The hat, coat, and pants are filled in with grey icing, the shoes in black, cuffs and trim in white using a No. 3 tip. The grapes are made with No. 2 tip using blue icing. The gourd is done in green with a No. 3 tip. The pumpkin is piped in orange using No. 5 tip and corn in yellow using a No. 3 tip. A No. 65 tip is used for the leaves.

CORNUCOPIA CAKE

Ice cake in light orange as shown. Cornucopia is filled in with a No. 8 tip in brown icing. Grapes are made in purple with a No. 3 tip. Apples, bananas and pears are piped out with a No. 5 tip. Happy Thanksgiving is printed on in brown icing with a No. 3 tip.

VALENTINE HEART

Cake is iced in white icing. Cherubs are piped in using the No. 6 tip with yellow for the hair and arrow and red for the heart. "Be my Valentine" is written in with a red icing using a No. 3 tip.

Lattice work as it is normally done is time consuming and not too attractive. These lattice designs are quite unusual and may be used on a commercial basis. This should give you a completely new conception of lattice work and its possibilities. The heart and diamond design which is criss-crossed and bordered, then placed over a curved pattern is very common and consumes too much time. For this reason most of our small lattice is made of one continuous line.

Royal icing thinned down with egg white must be used for all types of lattice. An even, uniform flow of icing is obtained when a steady pressure is used on the cone.

SCROLL LATTICE

The actual size of this pattern, is 2, 5 and 3 inches, respectively. After the pattern is drawn on paper it is placed under a sheet of wax paper.

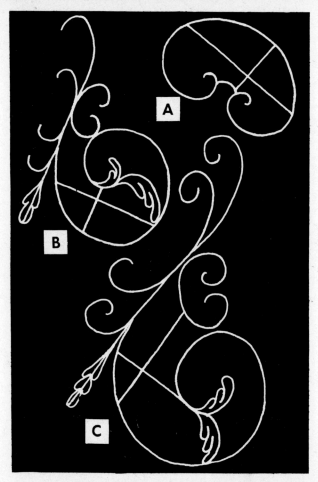

Using a No. 4 tube, fill a small cone with slightly thinned down royal icing. The lattice criss-crossed designs are first piped on the design. To maintain straight lines in your lattice, best results are obtained by lifting the tube off the pattern and letting the icing fall as you squeeze and move the cone across the design. The lattice should cross the pattern at a 45° angle in either direction. When this is completed the design is overpiped using the same icing with a No. 6 tube. The larger tube is desirable for the heavy outline of the pattern because this is the only real support of the lattice design.

Pattern B is a little more complicated. The lattice work is relatively the same but the overpiping requires a steady hand and pressure. *Pattern C* is almost the same except that it is smaller. Slip the wax paper to the side after completing the design, and use the same pattern to start the next piece of lattice work. They must dry for 24 hours, and in very damp weather, for 48 hours. When dry peel off the wax paper. These three types of lattice work are used around the tiers of a wedding cake. The larger lattice at the base, the medium sized lattice work above that, and the small lattice around the top. They are also used to construct various cake top ornaments,

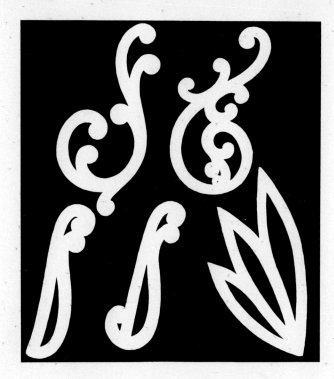

Lattice design No. 2. A large cone filled with royal icing and with an opening of about 3/16th of an inch was used for these designs. After the pattern is drawn out, it is stuck to your pan under a sheet of wax paper. In making the first design we begin at the base with a steady pressure and move the tube up and down to obtain the three peaks. When the overpiping is finished slide the wax paper over and using the same pattern, make another design. This method is continued until the wax paper is full.

This is the most practical of all designs because of its simplicity and the speed with which it may be executed. The next two designs are a little more complicated. The piping is started at the top and with one steady motion move down and finish the large curve. The other two smaller circular curves are then worked in. The last two designs are the smallest. They too are started at the top and are made in two movements as illustrated. These sections of lattice work are made up ahead of time and allowed to dry for 24 hours on wax paper. The lattice may be stored directly on the sheets of wax paper.

Lattice design No. 3. This design is similar to the one above. After the design is completed the wax paper is placed in a curved tin such as a one gallon can.

After drying, the wax paper is peeled from the lattice and a curved effect is obtained. The second piece of lattice work was completed in this way.

Lattice design No. 4. The six designs illustrated are very simple, and most of them may be made in two motions. All are started at the top. With a steady, even pressure continue down and around following the pattern. The "S" design must be started at the base and then simply follow the *S* pattern. If a very slow movement is maintained, the lattice will have tiny crinkled marks that are not desirable.

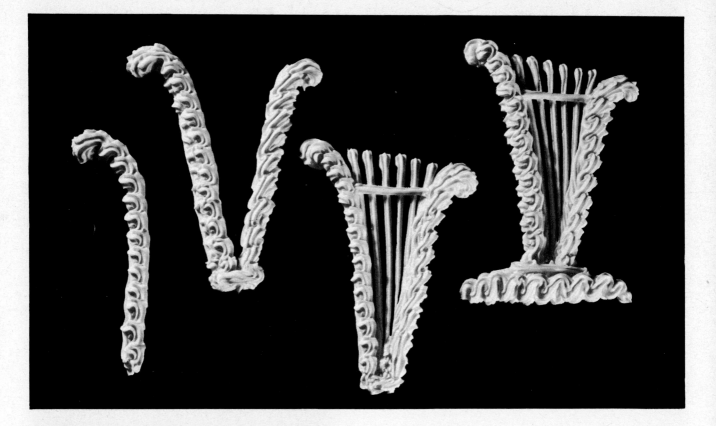

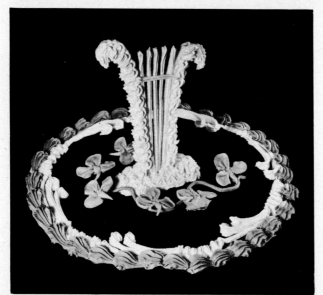

Lattice lyre. Use a large cone with a No. 16 tube and filled with a thinned down royal icing. With a circular motion the outside of the lyre is filled in. The six heavy lines are dropped in starting from the top and working to the bottom. One line is used to cross the lyre at the top as illustrated. The base is then piped on and is left to dry for 24 hours. The same procedure is followed for the opposite side after peeling off the wax paper. The lyre may be placed upright on a cake or used around the sides of a cake. Using this same method, numerals of any desired shape may be made and after drying placed upright on cake tops.

ELEPHANT STYROFOAM CENTERPIECE

This graceful beast of the jungle stands 12″ high and is 17″ in length. The top carriage is 8″ high and 9″ long. This is another piece available in Wilton patterns. Lay the pattern on the styrofoam sheet and trace the elephant as illustrated. The large ear may be cut separately and placed on the head using straight pins to stick it to the base. The carriage is then cut out and two dowel rods are used to attach the upper part of the carriage to the carriage base.

The elephant was trimmed with a thinned down grey colored icing using a small amount of black for the grey effect. This icing may be brushed on with a small 1″ wide brush. The trim was done using a No. 16 star tip and the fine scroll design was done with a No. 2 tip. Because this old guy is quite heavy, an 8″ styrofoam triangle was cut out, one side fastened to the back of the elephant and the other side fastened to the base, using 2″ nails to secure the two together. Green colored sugar was used for the base to simulate the grass. Seeing this old boy has been tamed, and put into captivity, the two young dancing girls are quite appropriate gazing out of the top of the carriage.

THE OLD WOMAN IN THE SHOE

There was an old lady who lived in a shoe. She had so many children she didn't know what to do. Using the Wilton styrofoam pattern, lay the pattern on ½" styrofoam and trace using carbon paper directly on the styrofoam. Cut all the sections with a styrofoam cutting knife and stick them together using straight pins. After the shoe, steps, chimney, roof and etc. are assembled, place the shoe on a styrofoam base. For a hilly effect use pieces of scrap styrofoam and cover them with icing and sprinkle with green colored coconut over base and all to give a life like appearance. The heel and sole of the shoe is made using a No. 5 tip. The heavy outline showing the shoe design is made

using a No. 30 tip. The window trim and shoe eyes are made with a No. 5 tip. The chimney and rear steps are filled in with a No. 5 tip. A No. 104 tip is used to fill in the roof. The shoe is then dotted using a No. 10 tip. The dots are simply squeezing and relaxing pressure forming a slight ball of icing. The little well at the base of the hill is made of styrofoam using 3 styrofoam circles placed on one another and 2 small sheets of styrofoam forming the roof. The roof is covered with a No. 104 tip and the base of the well is filled wth a No. 5 tip. All of the little children playing around the shoe are small wooden Italian imported candle holders found in our catalog.

CHILDREN'S PARTY CAKE

OLD LADY IN THE SHOE

This cake was made up in layers, put together and cut out to form the shoe. The door was cut from cardboard, iced with royal icing. The fence, gate and trellis were made with a No. 16 tip in royal icing and piped on sheets of waxed paper. After drying, they were placed upright in sections using royal icing to fasten the sections together. The wooden base was iced and covered with a green colored sugar to simulate the grass. The little cherubs and inhabitants of fairyland were made of ceramic and may be obtained through our supply catalog.

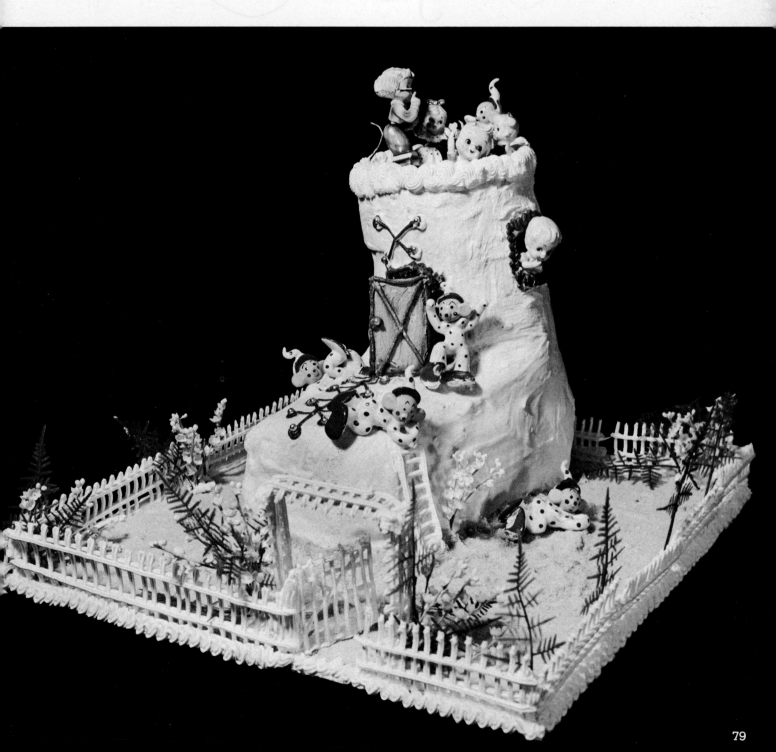

ROCKET CAKE

Here is a birthday cake the little guy will never forget. The cake base was baked in a 9″ round aluminum mixing bowl. The lower portion of the rocket was baked in a 4″ high tin can. The upper cone portion of the rocket was made of cardboard just as you would roll a paper cone. It was fastened together with the use of staples and the entire cake was then iced in a white icing. To keep the top section from sliding off the lower section a white dowel rod was pushed down through the two cakes. The border around the base of the cake was made with No. 6-B tip using a blue icing. This border was placed on at approximately a 45° angle. A large dragee was placed in the center of each drop flower border. The border directly under "Mike" was made with a No. 46 tip. The word Mike was printed in red icing with a No. 13 star tip. The stars were drawn in first, and then filled with red icing using a No. 2 tip. A small blue dragee was placed at the tip of each star. Directly under the fin of the rocket, the border was piped on in red, using a No. 13 tip. The four fins of the rocket were made in cardboard and iced with white royal icing. After sticking them into the side of the cake, they were trimmed in a blue icing using the No. 13 tip. The USAF was piped on with a No. 3 tip in red icing. The long lines running from the top to the bottom of the rocket were also piped on with red icing using a No. 13 tip. If you desired candles around the base they would be worked into the border itself as the icing is heavy enough to hold a candle upright. The two little rocket men on either side of the cake, were made of ceramic and would certainly make any little boy's eyes light up with delight.

SHIP AHOY

This cake was made for a child's party where a nautical theme was being used. The base was made from two layers of cake cut out forming the hull of the boat. The cabin was made of two layers of cake with one layer being used for the upper deck. The smoke-stacks were made of cardboard and iced in a dark blue. The styrofoam base was iced in blue and white icing using a spatula and swirl effect to simulate the water. The kids had as much fun scuttling and eating this cake as we had decorating it.

TRAIN CAKE

The train, coal car, two box cars and caboose were made using a loaf cake tin and cut to simulate the train. Large and small cookies were used and covered with icing and placed on as wheels. The railroad track was made in royal icing and gay colored lollipops were used around the outside for a colorful trend.

CALLA LILY ROSE ARRANGEMENT

This is a 9″ cake. The reverse shell is made with a No. 30 tip using pale green icing. The pitcher was outlined on the cake and then filled in. The calla lilies and roses are made up in royal icing. After drying, they are placed on the cake top as illustrated. "Easter Greetings" is written with a No. 2 tip using dark green icing. All flowers are described in detail in "Homemaker's Pictorial Encyclopedia of Modern Cake Decorating."

CORNUCOPIA

This is a 9″ cake made up of two layers, iced with a thin coat of butter cream and poured with a thinned down fondant. The fondant should be heated slightly before pouring. The cornucopia is made in gummed paste. After the cornucopia dries, the weave effect is made with a No. 46 tip. The green vine working around the side of the cake is made with No. 3 tip and the leaves are piped on using a No. 67 tip with a pale green icing. The directions for fondant and marzipan are given in our "Homemaker's Encyclopedia of Modern Cake Decorating."

CHRISTMAS SPRAY

This is a two layer 9″ cake. The cake is iced in white. The borders are done in a pastel green using a No. 22 tip. A spray of leaves and holly berries are piped on the cake with green icing using a No. 69 tip for the leaves and a No. 8 tip for the berries. The pine cones are made on a No. 7 nail in a similar manner to the American Beauty rose. Using the No. 104 tip and dark brown icing, first the center is built up just as for a rose and then flat squared off petals are worked around the center forming the pine cone. "Christmas Greeting" is written with a deep red icing using a No. 2 tip.

EASTER LILY CAKE TOP

This is a 9″ cake iced with white icing. The shell border is made with the No. 20 tip in a pale yellow icing. The Easter lilies are made with a No. 12 Easter lily nail in royal icing and are described in detail in our "Homemakers Pictorial Encyclopedia of Modern Cake Decorating." The perky chick is piped in yellow using a No. 5 tip. "Happy Easter" is written with a No. 3 tip in a deep green icing.

INTRODUCTION TO GUM PASTE

Gum paste is nothing more than cornstarch, powdered sugar, gelatin and water. When this mixture is worked together properly it has the consistency of pie dough and may be handled in much the same way as clay. It can be rolled out on a table in thin sheets and cut into various forms and patterns and left to dry. After drying, the various pieces may be placed together with royal icing to form any particular desired pattern. Gum paste may also be molded into various designs and shapes by using plates, glassware, or silver trays for patterns. Using patterns and molds with very little free hand work, gum paste work becomes child's play. Many of your own original ideas may be created in gum paste. By adding a few drops of peppermint to your gum paste, the gum paste will taste much like a mint lozenge when dried completely.

WESTMINSTER ABBEY

This is an actual scaled model of Westminster Abbey. It was constructed of Gummed Paste and is typical of the fine work that can be done in Gummed Paste.

GUM PASTE RECIPE

¼ oz. of gelatin (1 envelope equals ¼ oz.)
½ cup water
1 level teaspoon cream of tartar
Place on low heat and stir. When dissolved add four cups of powdered sugar, one cup of cornstarch.

Work like pie dough.
After mixing well in a bowl, cover with a damp cloth.
Gum paste handles much like pie dough.
Cornstarch is used for dusting the table to prevent sticking.

SMALL GUM PASTE BOWLS

To make some of the objects illustrated here, the table was first dusted with cornstarch. A small piece of gum paste is placed on the table, patted out slightly by hand and dusted with cornstarch on top, then rolled with a rolling pin to about ⅛″ thickness. The mold that you use is then dusted with cornstarch. The rolled out gum paste is forced into the desired mold. A sharp instrument is used to cut around the mold, and the gum paste is allowed to dry in the mold for approximately 12 hours.

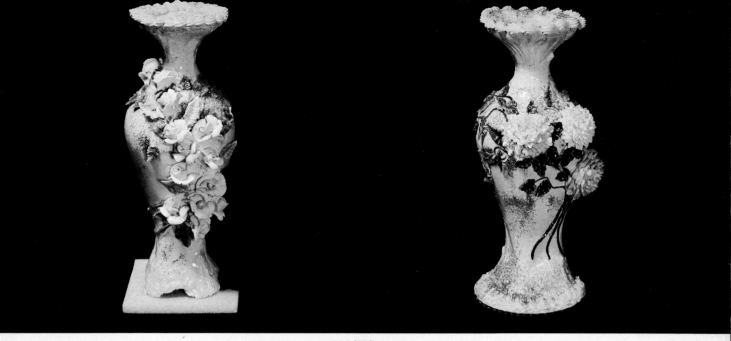

VASES

Two vases, made from gum paste are approximately 12″ high. After the vases dried a spray of half roses are worked around one vase and a spray of carnations placed on the other. The flowers are made up ahead of time in royal icing and placed on after drying.

LARGE VASE

A large ceramic vase mold was used for this mold. The mold was dusted in cornstarch. The gum paste was rolled out and molded around the vase in two sections, the edges trimmed off and then left to dry for 24 hours. The two sections were placed together using royal icing and the tree and the birds were piped on with royal icing using No. 3 tip for the birds and No. 8 tip for the trees. The green foliage on the tree was painted on with icing as is described in detail under scenery painting in icing.

LARGE GUM PASTE BOWL

This large gum paste bowl is molded on a 10″ mixing bowl. After drying, the mold is decorated with royal icing roses and trimmed with a border as illustrated.

INSTANT FONDANT PATTIES

Instant fondant patties will be a real treat for your family, friends, and next party guests. It can be made up very quickly and very easily by following the instructions given below.

Recipe
1 lb. of 10X powdered sugar
5 tablespoons milk
3 drops of mint or peppermint oil

Mix all the above ingredients in a saucepan and place on a stove with a medium flame. Heat to a temperature of 140 degrees, stirring constantly. Patties may be made in one of the following methods: Dropped out of a professional patty funnel, spooned out, squeezed out of a triple wrapped parchment bag, using a No. 5 tip, or as we have done here, using our confectioners molds. The molds are greased slightly with shortening or butter and fondant is spooned into the molds. After cooling they may be dropped out by turning the mold upside down with a slight tap and decorated as illustrated. Wilton plactic molds or those molds shown below may be used with this recipe.

MOLDS FOR CHOCOLATE OR BAKING

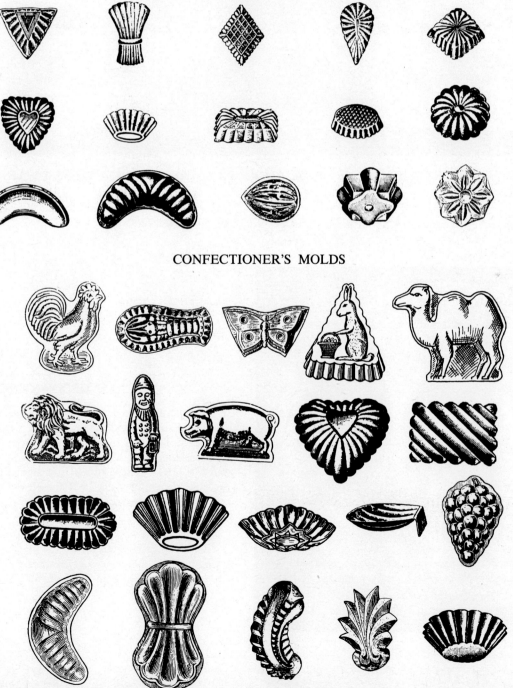

CONFECTIONER'S MOLDS

FONDANT PATTIES MADE FROM CHOCOLATE AND CONFECTIONER'S MOLDS

To dip grapes, strawberries and cherries or for covering petit fours, the fondant must be heated to a lukewarm temperature instead of the 140° temperature as for mints or molds.

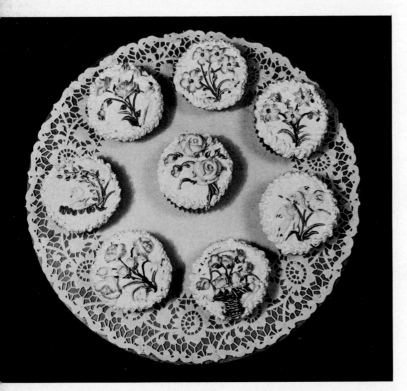

CUPCAKE DECORATING

In this picture are a few simple floral arrangements and floral sprays made especially for the tops of small cupcakes. The tips that were used are from a special small ornamenting set. The tips were No. 1s, No. 65s, and No. 101s. These are a tiny stem tip, a tiny leaf tip, and tiny flower tip. All the flowers, leaves, and stems were made in a boiled icing.

SHOW ME THE WAY TO GO HOME CAKE

This 14″ square cake was made up of three layers, each layer was iced in buttercream and placed in position. A small circular cut was made in the side of the cake and a bottle of champagne or grape juice placed in position as illustrated. The cake was iced completely with a white icing and trimmed in the following manner:

A No. 12 tip was used for the base border to form the pink balls of icing around the cake. The elephants were made with a No. 12 tip as illustrated. The icing used was pink boiled icing and it must be whipped up so that it is fairly stiff in order to hold its form. A long ball of icing was piped on the edge of the cake approximately 2″ long for the body. The four legs were piped in using the same tip, starting at the base of the oblong ball. We put the tip directly into the icing and started to squeeze and moved down approximately 1″ to form the right rear leg. This same procedure was followed

on all four legs. The head was piped on using a No. 12 tip. Starting with a heavy pressure at the top of the oblong body, moving down and relaxing pressure, the trunk was then formed. A short narrow tail was then piped on. The elephant ears were made with the No. 124 tip; starting at the side of the head, squeeze, move the tip slightly out and down, stop pressure and touch the side of the head. The legs and trunk of the elephants were trimmed in white boiled icing using a No. 4 tip and working in a small circular motion. After all the elephants were piped on around the side of the cake, as illustrated, one or two pink elephants were piped on climbing up the bottle.

The miniature cocktail glasses are available in various colors and were placed on the cake as illustrated. To simulate a drink in the glass, we filled them with colored piping jelly. These cocktail glasses are also listed in our supplies catalog.

BRIDAL SHOWER CAKE

This is a two layer 9″ cake. The cake is iced in a thin layer of butter cream and then poured with a white fondant. A No. 30 star tip is used for the shell border and also for the rope border around the top of the cake. The slipper in the center of the cake is made using the sugar mold method and comes from our No. 308 sugar mold set. The horseshoe worked around the slipper is first drawn in and then half roses and leaves are piped in, using the No. 104 tip and the No. 67 leaf tip. The tiny rose buds are made up ahead of time on waxed paper and after drying they are placed in the slipper which has been filled with a mound of icing as illustrated.

WEDDING SHOWER CAKE

This is a two layer 9″ cake. The cake was iced in a pastel pink and trimmed in the following manner: The base border is made with a No. 5-B tip. Each drop border has a No. 2 pink dragee in the center. The reverse shell around the top of the cake is made with a No. 22 tip. The three sugar bells going around the center were made with the sugar mold method using the No. WB5 medium sized bell mold. The small sprays of flowers winding between each bell were made with the No. 171 drop flower tip. The umbrella is a 9″ umbrella obtained from our cake decorating catalog. It was iced with a white royal icing and trimmed in pale pink using a No. 14 tip. The small pink circles were worked into the umbrella and topped off with a No. 2 pink dragee.

BABIES CAKE

Divide the cake in eight equal parts. A curved line is then piped in to connect the eight parts. With the use of a small cone and a No. 3 tip, fill in the criss cross lattice work. After it is completed, a No. 16 tip is used to finish off the lattice work, then overpipe with a No. 3 tip as shown. After writing the inscription, a small spray of apple blossoms and buds are added. The knitted baby bootie is described in detail in the "Homemaker's Pictorial Encyclopedia."

MOTHER'S DAY

This is a two tier 10″ cake iced in white butter cream and poured with a thin layer of fondant. The roses are made in royal icing using the No. 124 tip and after drying are placed on the cake in the following manner. First using a No. 3 tip and green icing and No. 67 leaf tip with green icing and striped with a very deep green along one side, the vine is piped on around the side and top of the cake. The roses are then placed in, and more leaves added. "Mother Dear" is written on a square of gummed paste that has the sides rolled up to form a plaque.

ILLUMINATED PLASTIC CHURCH

This dainty little church is perfect for a wedding cake ornament top for church affairs and for use during the holidays. The beauty and originality of the church is attained by trimming. The roof was decorated in brown royal icing using a No. 44 tip. Long diagonal lines were drawn out, cutting the roof at a 45° angle. After one side was complete, these lines or shingles were cut across in the opposite direction forming a lattice type church roof. The round simulated bricks of the church were made with a No. 5 tip using white royal icing. This is just a matter of a simple squeeze and stop motion making a round dot, and continuing these dots until the entire church, sides and front, were filled in. The fine trim around the church steps and windows were made with a No. 2 tip, using brown icing. The church was then placed on a small mound covered with royal icing and sprinkled with green colored sugar.

THE CROSS CAKE

The cross cake was cut from a 2 layer sheet cake. It was 14″ long, the upper portion of the cross was 12″ wide and the width of the cake was 4″. The cake was decorated around the base using a No. 21 star tip for the shell borders and a No. 16 star tip to trim off the top of the cross, using short back and forth motions. The cake was iced with white icing trimmed in a pale pink icing and decorated with large pink American beauty roses.

This cake would be ideal for Easter Time, Confirmation or other religious holidays.

ROYAL ICING CENTERPIECE

This centerpiece was used for a country club barn dance and was placed in the center of a buffet table. All of the guests were dressed in hillbilly clothes and we tried to simulate the theme for this particular setting.

A pattern was cut of cardboard for each section of the house. Each section was then made of royal icing in the following manner: A sheet of waxed paper was placed over a section and with a cone of royal icing and a No. 16 tip, a series of lines simulating logs were filled in until the pattern was completely covered. After drying for 12 hours, the sections were stuck together with royal icing. We used brown icing for the entire house and fence. A 12x18″ styrofoam base was used for the lawn and iced in thinned down green icing then sprinkled with green colored sugar. The swan was made using the sugar mold method. The flowers and trim around the fence were made of royal icing using bright yellow, pink, and blue flowers. Very little work went into this project but it was certainly a hit on the buffet table.

THE HONEYMOON HOUSE

Everything, we are sure, in a honeymoon house is certain to be sweet and this one is no exception. A cardboard pattern was cut and glued together to form the house. Miniature marshmallows were stuck on the cardboard using royal icing. The roof shingles were made of many colored candy wafers. The wafers were also used for the walk and the wishing well was made with the miniature marshmallows. The entire project was made on a 12x18 styrofoam base, iced in a delicate green and covered with green colored sugar.

GRADUATION CAKE

This five tier cake was designed by the Wiltons and decorated in class by the students. In commemoration of the 4,000th student graduating from the Wilton School, the ceremony has become a part of the tradition and is repeated at the graduation of every 1000th student.

A combination of two (specialty decorations) Sugar Mold method and Gum Paste was used to complete this five tiered cake which stood approximately four feet tall.

THE WISHING WELL CAKE

This cake was baked in our deluxe spring form pan which has a diameter of 9½ inches. After icing the cake, a No. 46 tip was used to trim the top. Starting on the outside and using a slight back and forth motion, the cake is circled completely. The second circle is made with the same tube using a contrasting color and so forth until the top is completed.

A No. 6 tip was used to form the bricks around the side of the cake. The top of the well was made in the following manner: Using ½″ styrofoam, six sections of styrofoam were cut out as illustrated in picture. The two large sheets forming the roof of the well were made from 9″ by 4½″ lengths. A 4½″ square of styrofoam was cut out and then cut into triangles. The supports holding the styrofoam top can be cut to any desired length. The Well handle and pulley were made by inserting a length of coat hanger through a ½″ square x 9″ length of styrofoam. The handle was shaped into a elongated reversed (L). The shingles on the roof were made with the No. 104 tip, starting at the base of the roof and moving in a straight line with a slight side to side motion. The next layer of shingles were placed slightly over the first layer and the same procedure was followed until the entire top piece was covered. The oaken bucket was made in royal icing using a No. 16 tip. The pale pink half roses were made up on waxed paper in royal icing. After drying they were placed on the cake, as shown. A cake such as this may be used for an engagement party, an anniversary and many other occasions.

BABY SHOWER CAKE

Which will it be, a he or she? Ribbons, booties, and bows all seem to ask this question. The cake was made from two 14″ layers. The lattice border on the top of the cake was made in the following way: Divide the cake off into 12 equal parts. A curved line is then piped in to connect the parts. With the use of a small cone using a No. 3 tip, fill the criss-cross lattice work. After this is completed, a No. 46 tip was used to go over the outside curved edging. The No. 46 tip was also used for the side border. A No. 4 tip was used to drop a guide line connecting each of the top borders. After this is completed a No. 46 tip is used in a back and forth motion following the guide lines. Three strings were then dropped into position as illustrated, using the No. 3 tip.

The base border was made with a No. 21 tip using a shell border. The top border is a reverse shell using the No. 22 tip. The tiny rosebuds were made up in royal icing on wax paper and after drying placed into position as illustrated. The small No. 67 silver leaves were worked into each cluster of rosebuds. The most important part of this project is the staff and crossbar which are used to hold the booties up. The total length of the staff is 17″. This was made from a clothes hanger and curved into the position as illustrated. The crossbar is 11″ long. After the desired shape is obtained, the wire is then wrapped with ½″ ribbon and bound in the center to fasten the crossbar to the staff. This is then stuck to the center of the cake.

Two 3¼″ circles were cut of ½″ styrofoam and attached to these circles are three ½″ wide ribbons. A straight pin was used to fasten each ribbon. They are brought up to the center and tied, as illustrated. The outside of the styrofoam base was then trimmed with a No. 104 tip using an up and down motion as you move along the outside of the styrofoam circle, thus forming a dainty fluted edge effect. The baby booties were made from our No. 302 Holiday set bootie mold using the sugar mold method. Each sugar bootie was trimmed in a contrasting color. A large ribbon bow was tied in the center of the staff and crossbar completing this most unusual baby shower cake.

PILLOW CAKE

Created especially for the Cinderella in your house The three layer 12″ square cake was cut down to simulate a pillow. The rope border was made with the No. 21 tip. The tassels on each corner of the pillow were made using the same tip starting at the bottom squeezing heavily, moving up and then relaxing pres-

sure. Large gold dragees were used to trim the four corners of the pillow. The clusters of half roses were made in royal icing using a No. 104 tip. The Cinderella carriage and the tiny dancing ballerinas are available in the Wilton Catalog.

RIBBON WEDDING CAKE

This cake consists of a 14″ square base made up of four layers, a 12″ round of three layers with an 8″ Grecian column separation sprayed in silver, and an 8″ three layer top. On this particular wedding cake we are not going to discuss the various border techniques. The unusual thing about this wedding cake is the original Wilton creation using bows instead of flowers. The cake should be iced in a boiled icing if the bows are going to stand over three hours on the cake. If a butter cream icing is used the grease or shortening would have a tendency to soak into the bows giving them a dulling effect. If all butter cream is used, the bows should be placed on at the wedding in order to maintain their high gloss. Four inch bows made of ½″ ribbon are used around the base. On the top of the second tier, we used three inch bows and cut the streamers into three sections, for a narrow dainty effect. For the top tier 2″ bows are used, and again the ½″ ribbon is cut into narrow streamers and placed on as illustrated. Carrying out the ribbon effect, in your cake top ornament, a series of 2″ bows are placed around the ornament base. A 3″ bow is placed on the top and streamers cut out and draped down over the sides of the ornament. We believe this new ribbon creation is very similar, at least in looks, to spun sugar work, and with this idea you may carry out many ideas in your cake decorating techniques.

APPLE BLOSSOM FLORAL ARRANGEMENT

This is a 9″ cake. The apple blossoms are made up ahead of time using the No. 104 tip with pink royal icing. The flowers are described in detail in our "Homemaker's Pictorial Encyclopedia of Modern Cake Decorating." The vine is piped on in brown icing using the No. 5 tip. The leaves are made with No. 67 leaf tip. The shell border is made with No. 22 tip in a pale pink icing.

HALF ROSE FLORAL ARRANGEMENTS

This is a two layer 9″ cake iced with a thin coat of butter cream and then poured with a thinned down fondant icing. The half roses are made in royal icing on waxed paper. The clusters or floral sprays are started about two inches inside the cake, and then brought down over the sides as illustrated. A No. 67 leaf tip is used for the leaves and a No. 4 tip for the line and stems.

BASKET OF FRUIT

The basket was made in gum paste rolled out with a rolling pin and shaped on the inside of a bowl. After drying, the basket was woven in brown and yellow using a No. 44 tip for the weaving and a No. 8 tip for the basket staves. Basket weaving was illustrated in our book "The Homemaker's Pictorial Encyclopedia of Modern Cake Decorating." Marzipan fruits and vegetables were made up ahead of time. They were also described and illustrated in the above mentioned book. The leaves and vines around the side of the cake were made with the No. 67 leaf tip and the No. 4 tip in pale green.

LATTICE BORDER DESIGN

This cake is divided in 8 equal parts. Then the arc outline is worked in, using a small cone with a No. 3 tip and the criss cross lattice work is completed. The outer edge of the lattice work is then completed with a No. 3 tip in a series of back and forth motions and is then overpiped with the use of the same tip. No. 16 star tip is used to complete the reverse shell. Simplicity in lattice completes this attractive design.

CLOWN FACE

This clown face and bust is one example of the many uses of boiled icing. The face is piped on using a No. 8 tip and smoothed down with a brush dipped in warm water. The hat is piped on with a No. 8 tip and trimmed with a No. 4 tip. The collar is made using the No. 104 tip. The boiled icing remains fairly soft so it cuts easily when serving the cake.

BIBLE CAKE

The Bible cake was baked in a 10"x14"x3" Bible cake pan. The cake was iced in white and smoothed out to a fine finish using a 2" brush dipped in hot water. The trim was done with a No. 3 tip. "Holy Bible" was written with a No. 3 tip, also the roses were made with a No. 104 tip in pale pink and artificial lilies of the valley were worked into the rose spray.

PARTY CAKE

This is a two layer 10" cake iced with butter cream. The comb effect is made with the decorating comb. The cake is then divided off into 16 equal parts using a No. 4 tip. The floral spray in the center of the cake is made in pale pink with white lily of the valley. Drop flowers and half roses are worked into the individual sections so when the cake is sliced, each person will receive a flower.

ROSE SPRAY

This is a two layer 9" cake iced in white icing. The shell border is made with a No. 22 tip in yellow icing. The scroll outlining the shell border is made with a No. 4 tip in pale green icing. For the rose spray a line is first piped on, using a brown and green icing with a No. 4 tip. The leaves are pale green and are made with a No. 67 leaf tip. The American Beauty roses are made with a No. 124 tip in yellow icing.

Introduction to

Wedding Cakes

Decorating wedding cakes in the home can be a very profitable business. Many homemakers have used our HOMEMAKER'S ENCYCLOPEDIA OF MODERN CAKE DECORATING as their only guide to this newly established business. The way to increase and maintain an outstanding wedding cake business is to give your customers something completely different . . . really beautifully decorated cakes.

You can decorate your wedding cakes as completely and as beautifully as the one shown here by the following instructions:

ASSEMBLING A THREE TIER WEDDING CAKE

A tier is made up of 3 or 4 layers of cake. A 3-tier wedding cake could have 9 or 12 layers, depending on the height you wish to make each tier. In this particular illustration, we have used a 16″ round tier made up of 4 layers, a 12″ round tier of 4 layers and an 8″ round tier of 3 layers.

Using a 20″ wooden cake board, cut silver doilies in half and place them around the board, fastening them in position with a small amount of royal or boiled icing. The 4 layer 16″ tier is placed on a 16″ corrugated circle and butter cream filling is spread between each layer. After the 4 layers are placed together, the entire 16″ tier is iced and placed on the 20″ wooden cake board. The weight of the next two tiers

will tend to push down into the bottom 16″ tier. By using dowel rods for support this will not happen. Dowel rods are ¼″ in diameter and 3 ft. long and can be purchased at lumber yards or hardware stores. After placing the 16″ tier on the 20″ wooden base, take a ¼″ dowel rod and push it into the cake until it touches the wooden base and clip it off level with the 16″ cake top, which will be approximately 5″ high. This is done 5 or 6 times forming a 11″ circle in the 16″ cake tier.

The 12″ tier, made up of 4 layers, is then iced in the same manner as the 16″ tier and placed on a 12″ corrugated circle. This tier is placed on the 16″ tier. The dowel rods which have been placed in the 16″ bottom tier will help support the 12″ tier. To keep these two tiers from shifting in warm weather 1 9″ long dowel rod is driven through the two cakes.

Before placing the 8″ partition on the 12″ tier, 4 dowel rods are pushed into the 12″ cakes and snipped off even with the top of the 12″ tier.

The 8″ tier of cakes is then placed on the partition. If no partition is used in a tiered cake, a dowel rod is sharpened at one end and driven down through the center of the entire cake. This is clipped off three inches above the top tier. After the cake is delivered the dowel rod is pulled out and the top piece is placed on the cake. This prevents the tiers from sliding out of place during delivery.

SIMPLICITY

This is a 12″, 9″, and 6″ cake. Each tier is made up of three layers. The cake is iced in butter cream and trimmed in a boiled icing. Three small clusters of roses are worked from the second tier falling down to the first tier. A styrofoam half moon is cut out and placed on the top using artificial lily of the valley in the center.

FOUR TIERED WEDDING CAKE

This cake consists of an 18″ square base made up of four layers, and a 14″ round tier, a 10″ Grecian partition, a 10″ round tier and a 6″ round tier. All round tiers have three layers. The cake is iced in butter cream and decorated in boiled icing. The pale pink roses are made up in royal icing and after drying are placed on the cake. Five silver leaves are worked into each rose cluster.

The attractive grouping in the center of the partition is made by cutting a 3″ styrofoam circle and inserting the stems of lily of the valley into this circle, and then placing the completed spray on the partition. The bells and the slippers are made using the sugar mold method. Around the square base of this cake are placed a string of 10 translucent roses with a tiny bulb in the heart of each rose which makes the final touch to this cake just heavenly. The entire string of translucent rose bulbs gives a delicate glow to the cake.

THE DUCHESS

This small two tier wedding cake, features a heavy cluster of roses between the tiers. The top piece is made of a heavy criss cross lattice work in royal icing and decorated with tiny pink flowers and leaves. This type of lattice work must be made up ahead of time on waxed paper. After drying, it is placed into position and decorated.

PRINCESS DEE

This cake is a 12″ base, 9″ and 6″ cake with a partition between the two bottom tiers. Four large clusters of Easter lilies and tiny drop flowers are worked between the partitions. The top piece is made of a cluster of roses with tiny white orange blossoms and lily of the valley placed behind the bride and groom. The entire top piece is finished off by placing rosettes of fine netting behind the cluster of flowers with royal icing.

FLORAL DESIGN

This is a 14″, 12″, 9″, and 6″ cake iced with butter cream and decorated with large American Beauty roses made with No. 124 tip in royal icing. All of the flowers are made up ahead of time and after drying are worked into the cake as illustrated.

THE CAPRICE

This cake has an 18″ square base tier with a 14″ round tier, a partition, an 11″ round tier and an 8″ round tier. A horn of plenty made by the sugar mold method is placed in each corner of the cake. Pastel pink roses and lily of the valley flow out of the horns. Instead of using the bride and groom, the top piece is a gum paste vase filled with tiny flowers, lily of the valley and leaves.

THE LADY WILTON

This cake is made up of 14″, 11″, and 6″ tiers, with partitions under each tier. The unusual thing about this cake is the ribbon effect under each tier, which gives the cake a very dainty appearance. The lattice work design on the sides of each tier are described in detail under lattice work. A tipped sugar bell made with the sugar mold method is used for the cake top piece.

PRINCESS

This variation is a 16″, 14″, 11″, and 6″ sized cake. The lattice work around the base of the cake is described in detail under lattice work. The swans in the corners are made of gummed paste. The cake top ornament is made using the sugar mold method and then placing on a 6″ swan partition.

PRINCESS

This variation is a 16 inch, 14 inch, 11 inch and 6 inch size. The lattice work around the base of the cake is described in detail under *lattice work*. The swans on the corners were made of gumpaste. The cake top ornament was made by the sugar mold method and is described in detail under *wedding cake top pieces*.

FIFTIETH ANNIVERSARY CAKE

This three tiered cake may be completed without too much labor. The cake is bordered with simple and quickly produced borders. The tiny yellow flowers dropped around the second tier are made with a No. 190 drop flower tip. You may recall it is made with a simple squeeze and turn. These are made up ahead of time and placed on the cake after drying. The small bells below the top tier are made with the sugar mold method and dipped into gold dragees. Around the base of the cake large yellow wild roses are worked in with gold leaves. The numeral "50" is made of gum paste and bordered with tiny yellow flowers. After drying it is placed upright on the cake with royal icing. A bed of yellow roses is worked around the base.

25TH ANNIVERSARY CAKE

We are not going to concern ourselves too much with the various type borders on this cake. The thing that concerns us is the particular layout and the use of some new type trim.

The 25th anniversary wreath is 5½″ high and is placed in a circle of silver crown. The top tier is trimmed with running tiny silver cherubs—the second tier has the double angel. The base of the second tier is wrapped with our new silver crown strip which is 1½″ high and comes in 20″ lengths. The bottom tier has an individual silver crown between each border. The tiers of the cake are 12″, 9″ and 6″. All tiers are iced in boiled icing, and the decorating completed in boiled icing. We spread silver lace doilies on a 16″ square wooden base to serve this cake from.

TUK-N-RUFFLE WEDDING CAKE

This 5 tiered creation stands almost 4 ft. high. The cake was iced in a delicate pink buttercream and decorated with white boiled icing.

A 25 inch square wooden base was used in setting up this cake. The cake sizes and partitions used are as follows:

    20 inch cake—#500 14 inch Separator

    14 inch cake, 11 inch cake—#500 8 inch Separator

     9 inch cake, 6 inch cake.

Two layers of green Tuk-N-Ruffle were used around the base. Before placing the 14 inch separator on the

20 inch cake, draw a 14 inch circle and lay silver Tuk-N-Ruffle around the 14 inch circle. Place the separator over this. The same procedure is followed under the 8 inch separation. Many beautiful color combinations may be made up using our most unusual grease resistant Tuk-N-Ruffle.

The separators were sprayed silver, using a pressure spray can obtainable at any hardware store. The color scheme of white borders over a pink cake, using silver Tuk-N-Ruffle, silver colored separator and silver leaves make this cake beautiful enough for a Queen.

PINK ICE

(THREE TIERED WEDDING CAKE WITH AN 8″ SWAN SEPARATION)

The bottom tier is an 18″ base made up of four layers. The second tier is a 12″ base made up of four layers. The separation is an 8″ swan separator sprayed with a silver paint which may be purchased in any hardware store. The paint comes in either silver or gold in a pressurized can. The top tier is a three layer 8″ cake. The entire cake is iced in delicate pink butter cream icing. The decorations are made with a boiled icing using a small amount of glycerin to keep the icing soft. In decorating wedding cakes we prefer to start at the base using heavier borders and then working up. The border around the base is a large shell made with a No. 5-B tip. The side border on the 18″ tier is made with a No. 48 tip. The string work is made with a No. 6 tip. The reverse shell on top of the 18″ tier is made with a No. 32 tip. The second tier or 12″ cake is decorated around the base with a No. 5-B tip. The vertical shell is made with a No. 32 tip. The string work and side border on the 12″ cake are made with a No. 5 tip. The shell border around the top of the second tier is made with a No. 32 tip. The two top borders and string work are described in our chapter on borders. All shells are made using a No. 22 tip and the string work dropping down from the separation is made with a No. 3 tip. All of the roses are made in advance in royal icing and placed on the cake after drying. Silver leaves and artificial lily of the valley are worked into the spray or clusters of roses to give them a lifelike appearance. A large cluster of lily of the valley are placed in the center of the partition and pink roses with silver leaves are worked around the base of the partition. To complete the top ornament, pink roses and silver leaves are worked around the base. To make this cake a little more interesting and unusual, we have added one layer of chocolate cake into each tier. We realize this is a slight deviation from the all white wedding cake, but when the cake is cut, and passed around to the wedding guests, everyone will remember this unusual chocolate layered wedding cake and it is fun to do something a little different now and then.

TUK-N-RUFFLE CAKES

Tuk-N-Ruffle is a new creation designed and manufactured by the Wiltons. Each completed yard of grease-resistant Tuk-N-Ruffle contains 5 yards of lovely lacelon and ribbon in green, pink, orchid, blue, yellow, silver, gold or white.

A very plain cake can be made beautiful with Tuk-N-Ruffle simply by placing the Tuk-N-Ruffle around the cake and piping on a border—or by placing the cake right on the Tuk-N-Ruffle. See page 113 for a fine example of exquisite artistry in cake decorating using Tuk-N-Ruffles and icing.

CAKE TOPS
WEDDING · ANNIVERSARY · BAR MITZ VAH

STYROFOAM WEDDING TOP ORNAMENT

This top piece was cut in sections using ½″ styrofoam and a Wilton pattern. You will find that these sections fit together beautifully and this along with the other patterns are a joy to work with. Just the smallest amount of decorating wed needed to enhance the beauty of this simple but dainty top piece. The trim was done in royal icing using a No. 3 tip. The bride and groom is our modern bride and groom No. 597. For additional decorations, a small vine may be worked up either side of the pillars and tiny pink rosebuds and green leaves may be placed on in royal icing. Small pink tea roses may be worked into the base. We thought it best to leave it plain as it would give you a better idea of how to construct this styrofoam ornament.

WEDDING CAKE ORNAMENT

The styrofoam wedding cake ornament was made using the Bar Mitz-vah pattern as described in previous pages. The six point star of David and the two lions were eliminated from the top section. We used four medium sized bells made from the sugar mold method, and on either side of the bells, kneeling angels. The angels come in silver and are two by three inches high. The bride and groom, and flower girl sets are made of china and were appropriate for this particular wedding cake ornament. By doing a neat job in cutting out your pattern, little or no icing trim is necessary in completing a most beautiful wedding cake ornament or table centerpiece. This completed top piece stands approximately 14" high.

BAR MITZ VAH CAKE TOP

We have had numerous requests for something completely different in a Bar Mitz-vah Cake Top. Many hours were spent in working out this most unusual design. The series of patterns are available and are included in the Wilton styrofoam patterns. The entire Bar Mitz-vah top is made by tracing the pattern on ½″ styrofoam using carbon paper and very carefully cutting out, using a styrofoam cutting knife.

Place 7 of the "A" pieced on top of each other. Run a wire down through the center. This will act as a pivot point. Turn each piece approximately 1¼″ forming the steps. One section of "B" is placed on top of "A" to form a base for your Grecian columns. These pieces may be fastened together using long nails or Elmer's glue. This is a type of glue that does not eat into the styrofoam. After fastening these eight sections together, place them on a 10″ circle of styrofoam as shown in "C," forming the base and pedestal. The next step is to place 2 5″ Grecian columns on this finished base. Cut out 2 1¾″ squares of styrofoam and secure to the pedestal using Elmer's glue. The columns are then glued to these squares. Another "B" pattern is placed on top of the two Grecian columns and glued

into position. This forms the top section of the Bar Mitz-vah. Three styrofoam circles, 4″ in diameter, 2″ in diameter and 1½″ in diameter are then placed one on top of the other and attached to this top section. These may be glued together or fastened together with straight pins. The six point star of David and the lions are then secured to the top section using straight pins. The "D" pattern, which is two flat pillars is then secured to the rear of the top and bottom "B" pattern, making up the complete top piece. The Bar Mitz-vah boy is glued into position. The Bible "E" is then put into position at a slight angle as pictured using a straight pin to fasten it. The entire Bar Mitz-vah top piece may be used as is or it may be trimmed. We trimmed the Bar Mitz-vah with blue royal icing, using a No. 21 tip and worked a reverse shell around the base and with a No. 46 tip to trim the sides of the steps and around the top. The lions were filled in with blue icing using a No. 5 tip. Depending on the colors being used, you may spray the entire top piece with gold coloring from a pressurized can. There are 14 candles used on a Bar Mitz-vah—7 candles on the front steps and 7 on the rear steps.

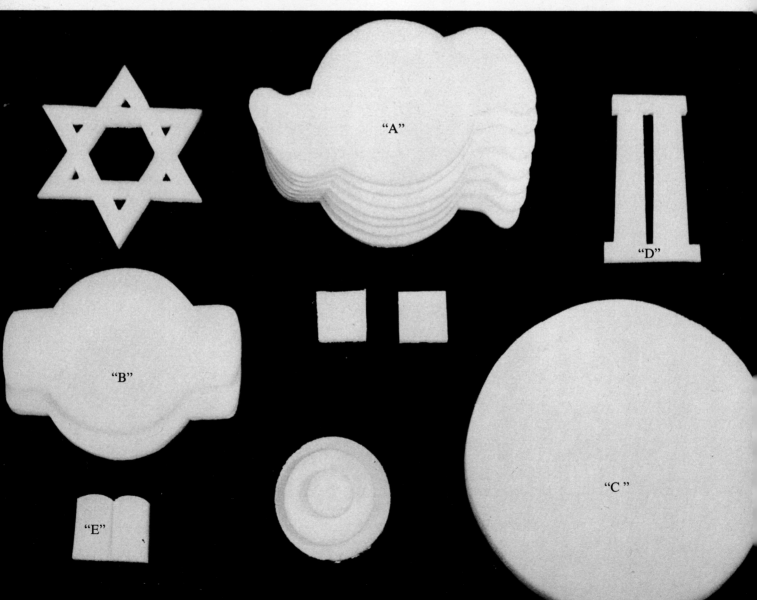

LATTICE CANOPY

Cut an oblong pattern from paper about 3 by 5 inches as illustrated. Using this for a guide, lay a piece of wax paper over it and with a No. 4 tube of thinned down royal icing complete your lattice work. After completing the entire design pipe a small border around the outer edge. Slide the wax paper from the pattern and follow the same procedure again. This completes the two side partitions of the canopy. The third and last section is made in the same manner. Immediately after completing the last section lay it over a curved object such as a small tin can bent in the proper shape. The four small lattice half moons used to simulate the gates are described under *Lattice Work*. At least 24 hours are required for drying. A 6 inch corrugated circle is then iced in royal icing and the three sections of lattice work are stuck together using royal icing. After drying the canopy is finished off with small pink rosebuds. Four rosebud clusters were used around the base with the vines climbing up the side.

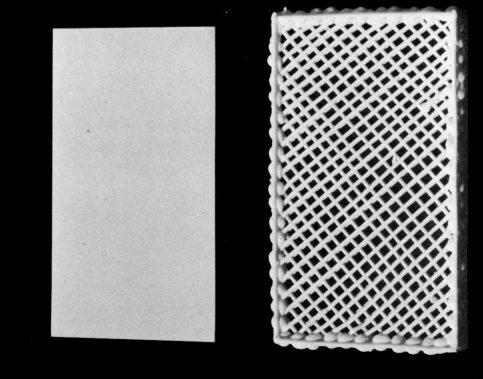

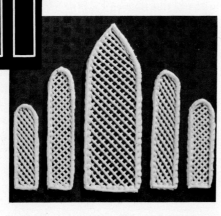

LATTICE CAKE TOP

Lattice Cake Top. These lattice cake top ornaments are made with a royal icing that has been thinned down with egg white. A No. 4 tube was used for the lattice design. This pattern was drawn first on paper as illustrated. A piece of wax paper is fastened down over the pattern. After completing the lattice work on each design, a small border is then piped around using the No. 4 tube. This border should be heavy enough to give the lattice work a sturdy outside structure. After the five pieces are completed they are allowed to dry for approximately 24 hours.

To complete the cake top a 6 inch corrugated cardboard circle is iced in royal icing. The large center section is peeled off the wax paper. Using the No. 4 tube, a strip of royal icing is then run underneath the base of this section and is fastened down to the 6 inch base. When attaching the other sections, the royal icing should be run down the side and the bottom of the section and then fastened to the first section of lattice. After the five sections are put together, they form a semicircle. These may be decorated further by working dainty roses around the base and putting a bride and groom in the center of the roses. If you wish you may fasten a cluster of tiny buds on either side of the lattice and work a small vine with buds and leaves climbing up the lattice work.

ANNIVERSARY CAKE TOPS

First draw the numerals. After you have designed the numerals to the desired size and shape, cut them out and use them as a pattern. There are two ways you may use this pattern:

1. Lay your pattern on a pan and stick a large sheet of wax paper over the pattern. Fill a large cone with slightly thinned down royal icing. Cut the opening to one quarter inch width. Fill in the pattern with the use of royal icing to a ¼ inch thickness. After drying for 12 hours, the numerals are lifted from the wax paper and turned over and overpiped on the opposite side. The drying process may be speeded up by setting your iced pattern on top of an oven or any other warm spot. A 6 inch circle is then iced in royal icing. The numerals are put in an upright position with the use of royal icing. These numerals may be decorated by working a very fine spray or vine of tiny flowers around them as shown.

2. Another method of making the 25 and 50, is by using gumpaste. Roll out to ¼ inch thickness. Then the patterns are cut out in gumpaste. After drying, stand them up by using a little royal icing.

These two methods of making numerals are standard procedures. A more practical way to do this is to cut the numerals out of masonite board ⅛ inch thick. The numerals are then painted with a thinned down royal icing, using a brush. These numerals are set up in the same manner as the gumpaste numerals. Using this method, there is no breakage and much time is saved by eliminating the drying process.

LATTICE CAKE TOP PIECE

This cake top ornament was constructed with five pieces of lattice work. A 6 inch cardboard circle is iced with royal icing. The five pieces of lattice work are stuck together back to back using royal icing. An inverted bell is then placed on the top of the ornament. Five bells are then placed at the base of the lattice work. The inverted bell on top was filled with drop flowers and leaves. A few lovebirds worked around the lattice complete this unusual cake top ornament.

SCENERY PAINTING IN ICING

The cake is first iced in a thick layer of butter cream and then poured with a warm fondant. Before painting the scene, the cake should set and crust for one hour. Scenery painting can be practiced on corrugated cardboard circles before attempting the actual cake scene.

A thinned down boiled icing and paste colors are used. In painting a scene such as the tropical scene, a picture may be obtained and copied in the following manner: With a brush approximately 1½″ in diameter, a small amount of thinned down boiled icing is placed in the skyline area. Using the brush in a back and forth motion, the skyline is painted in. Then with a tiny brush, place four or five small dots of blue, green or yellow paste colors in the skyline area. Using a larger brush and painting a series of back and forth motions gives the skyline a blue variegated effect. A large cone of brown icing is used for the landscape with No. 8 tip. After the icing is piped in, a brush is used with a little bit of water to thin it down and give it a rough mountainous look.

The water area is made by piping on a thinned down boiled icing and then adding a few drops of blue and green paste color. Using a large brush in a series of sweeping motions you create the greenish blue water effect. Use the deeper colors in the distant water. The palm trees are piped on with No. 7 tip using a brownish yellow color and the palm leaves may be piped on or painted on in green.

For the western scene, the sky is brushed in with white icing, a small amount of blue and then a few drops of yellow or orange tint or maybe a drop of violet. This is brushed in right above the horizon to give a sunset effect. The mountains are piped on then in white and brown icing. Using a small brush a few drops of deep colored icing are put on the crevices and then smoothed out with a larger brush. The cactus and tumbleweed are piped on with No. 2 tip and then worked out smoothly as the case may be, using a small brush with a little water.

The third scene showing the swans in the water are made very much like the above two, except the sky, was piped in first then the water, then the land using No. 7 tip. Each are brushed out smoothly. The tree is piped in with a No. 8 tip and then smoothed out with a brush. The leaves are piped on with No. 65 leaf tip and then worked out with a brush using a small amount of green or yellow color. The swans are then piped on in white.

KNICKKNACK PARTY CAKE DECORATING

The following pages are devoted to decorating cakes using ceramic knickknack types of ornamentation. These are worked into the cake top or icing to completely decorate a cake.

Any housewife can complete and follow the cake design even though it may be her very first attempt.

We carry an assortment of ceramics and decorative gold and silver special cake decorating trim.

BUTTERFLY CAKE

We've even sprinkled stardust onto gossamer wings as our pastel butterflies hover over the festivities! Lilies of the valley wind their way around candles ready to blend their radiance with the warmth of the occasion.

ANNIVERSARY

They strolled hand-in-hand through a fragrant spring garden and brought back this bouquet—to share with you! We've set it in styrofoam and strewn frothy pink mist all around. And then, as an extra, we wish them good luck.

GRADUATION CAKE

This gracious graduate clutches her diploma, and smiles, ever so slightly as she steps into the future. Her white and gold cap and gown blends with the lily of the valley at her side and the golden instruments add notes of grandeur to the occasion.

MINIATURE JAPANESE LANTERN DANCE

Every young lady from three to eighty-three loves to dance. Especially in this setting of Japanese lanterns. They are 2½″ across on 8½″ bamboo shoots in beautiful color assortments. All of the dancing is taking place on an 8″ two layer cake iced in a very pale yellow.

BALLERINA

With just a little coaxing, she twirls round and round to show you that her skirt is pretty—perky—and pink! A pastel rose and touches of gold touch off the highly glazed arch with glamour. A very proper setting for our beauteous ballerina. Swirling of icing around the base and top was done with a No. 8 tip. A squeeze and a twist form the soft fluffy blooms. Artificial pink roses were placed around the top of the cake and the candle arch with holders complete this lovely birthday cake.

FLYING STORK CAKE

These fellows look as though they were coming in for a landing, with their white wings spread and securely tied bundles in their bills. The plastic storks are mounted on 5″ pipe cleaners and gaily colored parasols add to the attraction of this 8″ fluffy pink cake.

ANGEL CANDLE CLIMBERS

Lifelike figures complete with pony tails and wings 4″ tall, will slide over any 8″ or 10″ candle. For our cake, we used two 8″ candles and pushed them into the cake to the desired level. This 8″ cake was iced in yellow boiled icing. A silver crown strip was placed around the base of the cake and the white border was made with a No. 22 tip. Artificial miniature yellow jonquils were placed around the top to complete this dainty arrangement.

ANGELIC PAIR

This is just right for a bridal shower...boy and girl are both robed in white with touches of gold and glittering rhinestones set in a pink rose are tucked in her hair. They are hand painted ceramic and the wooden bench they are seated on is painted dark green. You can make an arch like ours out of styrofoam. They are making love on a 10″ square cake and the silver gothic fence encloses them daintily

SHOWER

Which will it be—a he or a she? There's nothing sweeter than a baby girl—unless it's a baby boy! And here they are—fondling little lambs, patiently watching you open the shower gifts. And for the ethereal touch, add a few fantasy flowers.

CIRCUS CAKE

Begin by cutting a circle of cardboard the size of your cake and cover with aluminum foil (we drew it on), and mark off the center of the circle. From the center, draw a straight line to the edge and then cut along this line...by overlapping the two ends that you have cut and stapling them together, you form a slight cone effect. Use a No. 16 tip for the trim on the circus cake top. The cake is frosted in a gay color and the icing swirled, using a spatula. A No. 30 tip is used for the top border and the base is trimmed with a No. 190 tip. Drinking straws are used to support the circus top and tapered candles are placed in the bottom border.

EVERYONE LOVES A CIRCUS

They will come from far and wide to see this really different party cake. We placed one animal on each 4″ by 6″ cake...Striped soda straws stand upright around the cake and are fastened with straight pins into a styrofoam square top the same size as the cake. For a real big show, we topped the animal cakes with gaily colored clowns.

INHABITANTS OF FAIRYLAND

These spritely little red and white dotted elves scamper all over the cake and even tumble down the sides! They add gaiety to a children's party with their bright coloring. Our 9″ cake was decorated with a ready mix white icing and by using a spatula to give a swirly effect. The border around the base was a series of brightly colored balls piped on with a No. 8 tip. The long tapered candles were placed in the center of tiny little toast glasses. A cake the kiddies will never forget.

RING UP THE CURTAIN

It is time for the next act to begin. The youngsters will have a circus with these brilliantly colored clowns, and will keep them as a constant reminder of a wonderful party. We used a No. 8 tip and made little swirls of icing for the balloons. The magic ring candle holders are shiny nickel plated and brightly colored candles circle the cake.

STYROFOAM CONFECTIONS FOR FUN AND PROFIT

The Wiltons have developed a completely new method of decorating using styrofoam as the base and trimming the center piece with royal icing. We have developed 17 styrofoam center pieces. Each is drawn out to exact size and is in sections. The 17 patterns are available in our cake decorating catalog.

CLOWN CENTERPIECE

This colorful clown stands 15″ high and was made using the Wilton clown pattern. Lay the pattern on a sheet of ½″ styrofoam and trace over carbon paper. Cut with our styrofoam cutting knife or similar sharp object. The sections are then placed together using straight pins. After this is completed, stand the entire clown upright on a base of styrofoam 6″x11″. Four 2″ nails may be used and pushed up through the bottom of the styrofoam to fasten the bottom of the clown to the base. If you have a little difficulty in fastening the clown to the base you may cut out a 7 inch triangle, fasten this to the base, and the one side of the triangle to the back of the clown. For all the styrofoam decorations, the icing used was a straight royal.

Starting at the top of the clown, the tassels of the hat were made with a No. 3 tip, while the ruffle around the hat was made with a No. 104 tip using an up and down motion as you move the tip along. The facial features were put on with a No. 2 tip and the rest of the face filled in with a No. 3 tip. The ruffle around the collar was made with a No. 104 tip. The hands were filled in with a No. 3 tip. The ruffle around the sleeves was made with a No. 104 tip. The clown's body and arms were filled in with a No. 9 tip. The polka dots were also made using a No. 9 tip. The oversized shoes on the clown were made with a No. 104 tip. The styrofoam base was then covered using a No. 48° tip.

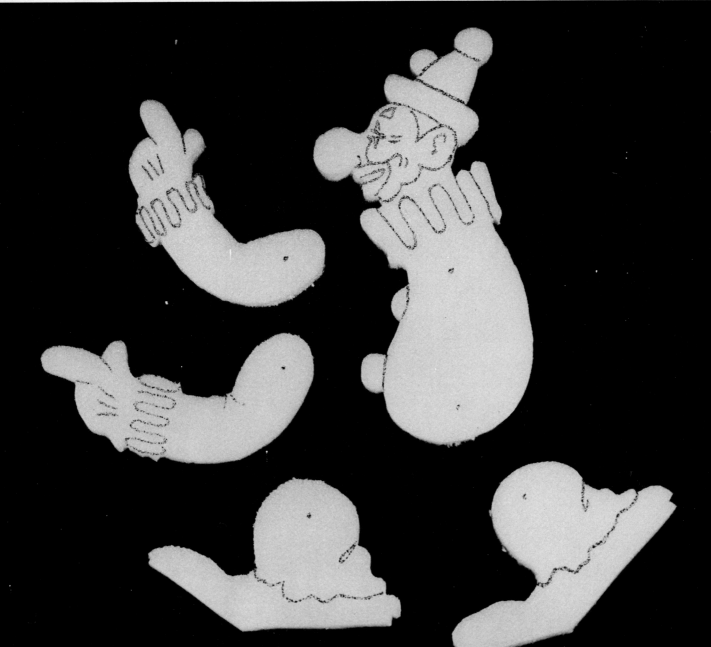

THE GIRAFFE CENTERPIECE

The giraffe stands 18″ high and was made of ½″ styrofoam. The base is 12″ by 6″ and the entire project was made in the following manner. Using the Wilton styrofoam pattern, trace giraffe using carbon paper and drawing directly on the styrofoam sheet. The giraffe's legs and tail are fastened to the body using straight pins. Place the giraffe on a styrofoam base and use 2″ nails sticking up through the base into the legs to secure the two together. The face is filled in using a No. 3 tip. The body is a series of icing dots made of royal icing piped directly on the styrofoam. You may pipe the brown spots out first and then fill in with the white. The styrofoam base was covered in green icing and then sprinkled with a green colored coconut. The sides of the base were filled in with a No. 104 tip using a back and forth motion.

PETER COTTONTAIL

My, what fun we had making this jolly Easter bunny. One look at him and you expect the little guy to hop right off the table and he may do just that if you don't secure him tightly to the base, using 2″ nails stuck up through the base and into the bunny as previously described for assembling styrofoam characters. Using the Wilton styrofoam pattern, lay the pattern on a sheet of ½″ styrofoam and trace the various sections directly on the styrofoam with carbon paper. The various sections are stuck together using straight pins or one inch nails. The entire bunny is decorated in royal icing using No. 14 tip. The fill in method is simply a series of dots, squeezing and relaxing pressure until the bunny is completed as shown. We suggest that in decorating and cutting out this bunny you make it a family project because it is certainly simple enough so that all hands may participate.

THE STORK CENTERPIECE

With this cheerful looking bird standing in the center of your shower table, you are certainly sure to thrill your guests and become the talk of the neighborhood. Cut stork out of ½″ styrofoam using the Wilton pattern. The legs are made with two thin dowel rods ¼″ in diameter and 7 inches long. The dowel rods are stuck into the styrofoam spats and into the base for support. The neck and body are fastened together with straight pins. The hat can be shaped from 4½″ pieces of styrofoam cut in an oval shape 3″ long and 1½″ wide and pasted together with a circle of cardboard for the brim. Royal icing is used to decorate the stork. The hat was filled in using a No. 16 star tip with a slight back and forth motion to make up the design. The neck and bill are piped on with the fill in method using the No. 24 star tip. This is accomplished by simply making a series of squeezes and stops or dots until the entire styrofoam neck is covered with icing. A leaf tip is used to fill in the body, drawing out long leaves starting at the tail and working forward. Either a No. 71 leaf tip which is quite large or a No. 67 leaf tip can be used. The 2 dowel rods which are used for legs are filled in with a No. 24 star tip using a series of dots as described above. The spats are filled in also using the No. 24 star tip and the base is filled in with icing using the same tube. The overall height of the stork is 21 inches.

FIRE CHIEF

This ladder leads straight to enchantment for some little boy, and a world of recognition for you—it's made of drinking straws. It rests against a 9″ two layer cake that is frosted in either boiled or buttercream icing... brick markings are made with a No. 3 or No. 4 tip in a deep color. Chimney is made from cardboard paper holder cut down, and frosted and decorated the same as the cake.

LONG JOHN SILVER PIRATE SET

WHAT LITTLE BOY WOULDN'T be thrilled to have these four colorful, ready for action pirates invited to his party? They leave their ship with full blown sails in the background and spill their gold (foil covered Danish chocolate) as they charge ahead, all set to make this cake a never-to-be-forgotten one!

KNIGHTS OF THE ROUND TABLE

A 9″ birthday cake decorated completely with our silver and gold embossed figures. The top and bottom border were made with a No. 22 tip using a fluffy boiled icing.

RURAL LIFE KIDS

Ideal cake top decorations are made with these Rural Life Kids Salt and Pepper shaker assortments. Dolls are trimmed with gold lace; the pussy willows are in pale green and the base of the cake trimmed with silver crown strips. Drop flowers and reverse shell border complete the cake.

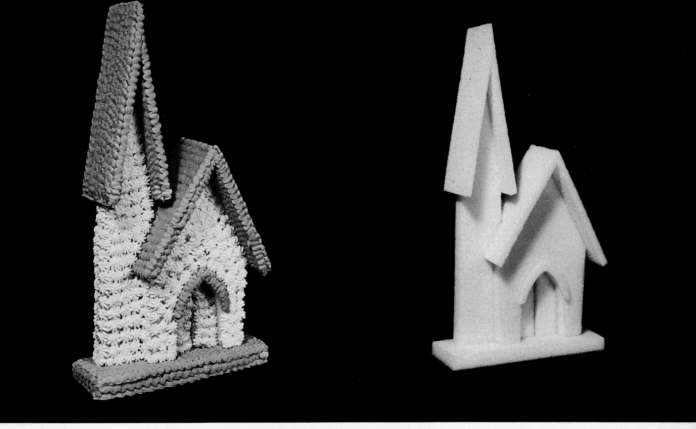

STYROFOAM CHURCH FRONT

Using the Wilton pattern, the styrofoam church is cut out of ½" styrofoam and put together with straight pins as illustrated. The church front is decorated in royal icing using a No. 22 tip. The trim on the roof and the base is made of pastel blue icing using a No. 46 tip. Starting at the top and moving down in a straight line a slight back and forth motion is maintained as you follow the roof from the top to the lower section. This is repeated until the entire roof is filled in. The same procedure is followed on the base. A centerpiece such as this may be used around Christmas time or for a small wedding party. A bride and groom may be placed in front of the open door for a shower or wedding centerpiece.

The overall height and width of this church is approximately 16"x9".

HANSEL AND GRETEL STYROFOAM HOUSE

Using the Wilton pattern, the 4 sections of the house and 2 sections of the roof are cut from ½" styrofoam. In your pattern you will notice the chimney, roof and overall shape of the house has a slanted irregular shape. This will help exaggerate the fairyland shape we are trying to show. The house is put together using straight pins. We use a No. 8 tip and royal icing in pink and white. Starting at the base of the house, a row of pink dots are worked around the entire house. These rows of dots may be alternated, the first row in pink, second row white, and so forth. The roof is shingled with pink and white icing, using a No. 104 tip. Starting at the lower section of the roof, the tip is moved along with a slight back and forth motion forming the shingle effect. The next row which was white is overlaid slightly on the first row, using the same motion. This procedure is continued until the entire roof is covered. A crooked chimney is made up in advance and set into the soft shingles at an angle. The house is set on a styrofoam base, which can be tinted with green icing and green granulated sugar. The fence is made using a No. 8 tip with any desired colored icing.

The overall dimensions of this fairyland house is approximately 10"x10"x8".

WEDDING CENTERPIECE

This pattern is available in the Wilton styrofoam patterns. The two moon sections were cut out of ¼" styrofoam and a length of cardboard was curved around the base of the moon and attached to either sections using straight pins. The moon was then trimmed with a pink icing using a No. 16 star tip. The face was trimmed with a No. 3 tip. Small artificial yellow jonquils and lily of the valleys were pushed into the styrofoam base. The styrofoam stars were stuck into thin wire and placed into position as illustrated. The centerpiece was then tied with a large pink and white bow.

HONEYMOON CART

This honeymoon cart has no pattern. We felt that after making as many variations as you have, it would be fun to try cutting out a few sections and putting them together on your own. You may use the horse pattern available with your Wilton styrofoam patterns. The various sections of the honeymoon cart are cut out using ½" styrofoam. The horse was trimmed with a light brown royal icing using a No. 14 tip. The cart was trimmed with bright yellow royal icing using a No. 3 tip. The bride and groom set comes in the sitting position as illustrated. On the back of the little cart, we had a large sign "Just married" printed in royal icing.

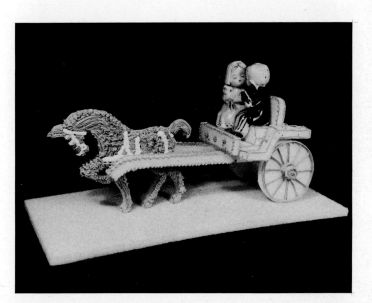

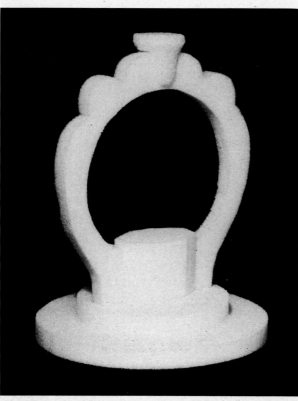

WEDDING RING SHOWER CENTERPIECE

Using the Wilton styrofoam pattern, cut the ring out of ½″ styrofoam. The ring is then attached by using 2″ nails which are pushed up through the styrofoam base. The ring is trimmed with a pale pink royal icing using a No. 3 tip. Number 3 dragees are worked into the top of the ring to simulate diamonds. Pale pink roses and silver leaves are used around the base of the ring, and a small cherub bride and groom ornament which is 2½″ tall is placed in the center of the ring. The overall height of the wedding ring centerpiece is 12 inches.

WEDDING SHOWER CENTERPIECE

This pattern is available with the Wilton styrofoam patterns. The wedding bells and bow were cut out of ½″ styrofoam. A 16″ long dowel rod was wrapped in pale pink ribbon and stuck into a styrofoam base. The styrofoam bow was stuck into the dowel rod and the bells were glued to the dowel rod using Elmer's glue and a few straight pins. The piece was trimmed off with a No. 8 tip using white icing and pale pink icing for the trim. The two doll faces were made from styrofoam balls trimmed in icing and the netting was glued on with Elmer's glue. A narrow stick approximately 7″ long was placed into the center of each ball, wrapped with pale blue ribbons and stuck into the styrofoam base, forming the completed centerpiece.

UMBRELLA TABLE CENTERPIECE

The umbrella pattern is available in the group of Wilton patterns. The umbrella stands approximately 16″ high and was cut out of ½″ styrofoam fastened together with straight pins. The base of the umbrella was stuck to the styrofoam base using 2½″ nails pushed up through the bottom of the styrofoam base into the handle. The umbrella was decorated in white and blue royal icing. A No. 12 tip was used for the white trim making a series of small back and forth motions and following the lines as illustrated. The fill-in method or large dots were piped on with a No. 12 tip in blue icing. The small trim around the base of the handle was made with a No. 4 tip.

SURREY WITHOUT THE FRINGE ON TOP

The two horses and surrey were made with a Wilton styrofoam pattern. The pattern was laid over a sheet of ½″ styrofoam and traced directly on the styrofoam with carbon paper. The sections were cut out with a styrofoam cutting knife and pieced together using straight pins. A No. 452 bride and groom ornament which is made in a sitting position on a bench was placed on the seat of the surrey and fits perfectly. The surrey was trimmed with a No. 14 tip, using a pale pink icing. The horses were trimmed with a pale yellow icing using a No. 14 tip.

OLD FASHIONED BUCKBOARD

Using the Wilton pattern, the buckboard was cut out in sections using ½″ styrofoam. This is a very simple piece and may be made by a child. The sections were put together with straight pins. Two prancing ponies made of ceramic were placed in position to pull the cart along. The buckboard was trimmed in bright yellow royal icing using a No. 3 tip. The wooden seat that we used was the bench from the bride and groom set No. 452, which was used on the Surrey centerpiece. The funny dressed clowns are 3½″ high and the legs and arms may be moved in any comical position. These are available in our catalog.

STYROFOAM CART WITH UMBRELLA TOP

Because of the simplicity of this piece we did not make a pattern. Simply cut out four, two inch circles for the wheels, two sides, front and back for a simple type cart. We used a 9″ umbrella iced with a bright yellow, sprinkled with silver dragees and we filled the cart full of tiny little flowers and lily of the valley. Pulling the cart we used four prancing ponies and placed them in a bed of delicate green colored sugar.

SHOWER SPRINKLING CAN

This pattern is available with the Wilton Styrofoam pattern sets. The completed shower can stands approximately 14″ high. The shower can was cut from ½″ styrofoam. The pattern is laid directly on the styrofoam and traced out using carbon paper. The can was trimmed in a pale blue royal icing using a No. 3 tip for the fine trim and a No. 103 tip for the heavier trim and also worked around the base as pictured. A centerpiece such as this is certain to be a hit at your very next shower. Why don't you try it and see.

DOLL STYROFOAM CENTERPIECE

This young lady stands approximately 17″ high and was made in 4 sections. Fasten the styrofoam sections together with straight pins and stand the doll up on a 10″ circle of styrofoam, using 2 inch nails stuck up through the bottom of the styrofoam and into the doll's skirt for support. The doll's hat was decorated entirely with royal icing using a No. 17 star tip to fill in the long parallel lines with a slight back and forth motion to create a design. We tinted the face with pink icing, smoothed out with a brush. The hair was filled in with a No. 3 tip. The blouse of the dress was filled in with a No. 17 tip. The arms and gloves were made using the brush method for a smooth finished effect. The ruffled edges of the doll's dress were made with a No. 104 tip. The lower section or lower three ruffles were made with a No. 124 tip. Pink roses and silver leaves were used around the base.

GREETING CARDS DECORATED IN ROYAL ICING

A new and fascinating idea may be worked out in decorating using greeting cards as designs to be followed. Using a white cardboard (in our case, black to show the design a little more distinctly), or heavy white paper, cut a card out to approximately the same size as a normal type greeting card. The decorating and inscription must be done in royal icing. This is a novel gift for your friends when boxed attractively. These are a few examples of some of the many ideas we believe will thrill your friends.

ICE CARVING

A number of our readers have requested information on the techniques of cutting simple designs in ice. The following ice pieces which we shall describe and talk about were cut from a 200 lb. block of ice. These were made in class by students during their first lesson. The four pieces pictured here took approximately three hours for two students, with Mr. Wilton instructing, to complete.

A pattern was first drawn out on paper of the particular design to be created. The pattern was then cut out, placed on the side of the block of ice and marked on the ice, using a sharp instrument. The carving of the ice is done with a small tool which has approximately 6 points of an ice pick spaced ¼″ apart. With a series of jabs or strokes, the design is then roughed out. Smaller tools which are approximately ⅛″ to ½″ in width and have a silght curve at the end are then used to form the more individual detail.

LARGE PUNCH BOWL

The punch bowl was hollowed out and a red light was cut into the base for an unusual effect.

CORNUCOPIA

This is a very appropriate buffet decoration and is used for meats or jello salad, placed around the base of the cornucopia.

The cornucopia was cut out as previously described. The base was marked in with a heated rod. Pictured by the cornucopia was one of our recent students, Mrs. Rita Komar who was very thrilled with her very first ice sculpture piece.

SWAN

The Swan was traced first on paper, cut out and then carved as previously described. The long feathers or lined effect in the swan were made using the flat rod. After heating, press against the ice, thus melting into the ice and giving the feather effect.

LARGE BASKET

The basket was cut out of paper, placed on the block of ice and then chiseled out as illustrated. In Mr. Wilton's right hand you will see the instrument that does the major part of the cutting. The diagonal lines worked into the base of the basket were made from a flat piece of steel heated over a gas stove and then pressed to the ice, melting the long lines. These are placed approximately 1½" apart and criss-crossed as illustrated. This basket was also hollowed out and may be used for fruit, punch or just as a centerpiece.

McKinley Wilton and Norman Wilton admiring the cake decorated especially for the occasion of the 200,000 edition of their world famous, best selling

"WILTON ENCYCLOPEDIA OF MODERN CAKE DECORATING"